Becoming Holy

(Without being Holier-Than-Thou)

A Brief Exploration of Franciscan Spirituality through reflecting on the Admonitions of St. Francis of Assisi

by

Karen S. Woods

Sleeping Beagle Books
Jacksonville, Illinois

ISBN # 978-0-9792832-3-9

Library of Congress Control Number 2008911833

Cover photo by Kevin Rosseel

This book is dedicated to Mary, *theotokos*, the patroness of the Franciscan Family.

This book is also given in fraternal love to all my Franciscan brothers and sisters.

Peace and Goodness!

Table of Contents

Author's Note

When I pondered titles for this small book, I immediately discarded B*ecoming Holy (without being Holier-Than-Thou)*, cringing, knowing some people would find that title to be hypocritical, presumptuous, and/or laughable, especially coming from my pen. And yet, gradually, the title grew on me, as those words condense the essence of what it is to live a Franciscan life: following Jesus in the footsteps of St. Francis.

Although Franciscans are penitents, our lives are joyful. There has hardly been a better display of the peaceful joy coming from a total abandonment of self to God than the life of Francis of Assisi. While it was Saint Paul who wrote "Rejoice in the Lord always" to the Philippians, Francis made that biblical advice his own. In *Mirror of Perfection*, chapter 25, a brother returned home joyfully singing the praises of the Lord. Francis remarked, that this is how he wished his brothers to be, "happy, both rejoicing and praising God."

I make the pretense to be neither a great Franciscan scholar nor a particularly holy person. Instead, I am, as most Franciscans have been almost from the very beginning of the Franciscan movement, a married person, a wife and mother, living out the Franciscan way, as best I can, in the world.

The Franciscan Charism, the unique spiritual gift given to us for the good of others, lies in a strong reliance on the sanctifying and actual graces of God to live out the Gospel of Jesus Christ each and every moment of our lives. We know each grace of God is a gift given freely to us out of His love for us. We have neither earned grace nor do we deserve it. But He is merciful and loving, always surprising us with His perfect gifts.

A lifetime commitment to penance and conversion of life that ever seeks to conform ourselves more closely to Jesus —of necessity—requires us to be open to the constant reception of divine grace in order to be the people we have committed ourselves to be. We receive grace in very many ways. Grace is, of course, received from the normal channels of grace: the sacraments of the Church. And yet, God's grace is like David's overflowing cup.

We find God's grace in many places, in the acts of corporal and spiritual mercy we perform as His hands in the world. We find grace in the muffled quiet of a nursing home at midnight as we sit with the dying. We find grace in the face of a homeless person as we give him a bowl of hot soup on a cold day. We find grace as we teach children the beauty of truth. We find grace as we find beds for the homeless, or build houses for those who have no homes. We find grace as serve the needs of others with as much joy and competence as we would ourselves wish to be served, if we were the ones in need of help.

Most of all, the Franciscan spiritual life is centered entirely on the adoration of, and deep personal friendship with, Jesus Christ, our Lord, true God and true man. Francis, in *Rule of 1221,* the Latin titled *Regula non Bullata (Rule without a Bull,* in English),* chapter 22, wrote, "In holy love, who God is, I ask all my brothers, ministers and others, to disregard every hindrance, to set aside all care and solicitude, and to serve, love and adore the Lord God with a pure heart and a clean mind, because this is what He seeks above all else. We must make in that place (within ourselves) a home and an abode for him who is the Lord God; Father, Son, and Holy Spirit."

The Franciscan life also possesses a deep admiration for, and patterning of our lives upon, the selfless devotion shown to Jesus by His Blessed Mother, Mary. Francis took the Blessed Mother of God as his patroness.

Fond of calling himself "simplex et idiota", simple and ignorant, Saint Francis was anything except those things. He was a man called by God to a great work, the work of rebuilding God's Church. It is a work that continues through the Franciscan family, even now. Francis had a great ability to remember the scriptures, although his scriptural citations are often more paraphrases than direct quotes from the Bible. Most of Francis' extant writings are peppered with scriptural references.

The Admonitions of St. Francis, which are the core of this small book, are twenty-eight items of spiritual advice Francis gave to his followers during his lifetime, most likely written down after he passed from this world into the heavenly realm.

There is a real spiritual wealth in examining these words of holy counsel and applying them to our lives. By no means are they easy to live with, but then again, they're nothing more than the implications of living a Gospel life. And it's never been easy to be salt and light in a world that would far rather be on a salt free diet and live in darkness.

Yes, the words were originally given to a group of celibate brothers who lived in community. There's an old Franciscan saying, "The world is our cloister." Franciscans have always been in the world, serving, preaching the Gospel, through our actions and our words, often more through our actions than in our words.

My prayer for all of us is that we can each grow in holiness, in righteousness, and, most of all, the profound humility, intense charity, and overflowing joy we need to have in order to work with our brothers and sisters; knowing as Saint Francis did that no matter how closely we seek to walk with God we can't close that distance between ourselves and God by either our own merit or efforts. Friendship with God is essentially a gift from God, offered by Him to us with open hands. It is God, Himself, who seeks us. The One who died for the love of our love, waits for us to return His love.

Francis knew this, and wanted us to love God with our whole heart, mind, soul, and strength. It was to this end that Francis urged his brothers and sisters. It remains our goal today; not personal holiness as an end onto itself, that we should boast of our accomplishments, but simply becoming more like Christ so that we can show His love more effectively, through actions more than in words, to a hurting world. Showing that love, we then can call the world to repentance, beginning as always with the Church. After all, God's initial call to Francis' from the cross of the Church of San Damiano was to rebuild the Church.

It is essential that we, as Christians, particularly as Franciscans, be encouraged and supported in the important work God has given us to do. Sitting at the feet of our Seraphic Father Francis, listening to his wisdom, is a good way of gaining strength and encouragement for the work we have before us.

Over the years, I've greatly enjoyed the gifts of time and of a desire to learn that the Lord has given to me. God gives gifts intending that we who receive those, in return, share the benefits of those gifts with others. So, sharing what I've learned so far during my Franciscan walk, so that you may be blessed, is my entire purpose in this small work.

As we read through *The Admonitions* together in this small work, I will first give the passage in Latin, then in as clear of English as I can accurately render it. Finally, I will offer a reflection on each passage tying it together with other Franciscan source material and scripture elaborating on that. All the translations given in this small book are strictly my own and original to this work.

The Latin text of the *Admonitions* presented here comes from Fr. Kajetan Esser O.F.M.'s *Die opuskula des hl. Franziskus von Assisi,* Neue textkritische Edition. Editiones Collegii S.

Bonaventurae ad Claras aquas, Grottaferrata (Romae) 1976. I'm also grateful to paxetbonum dot net for the Latin text of the early biographies of St. Francis.

My prayer for you as you read this small work is that you may find something here that helps you in your walk with Jesus.

Wishing you peace and goodness,

Karen Woods

Caput I: De corpore Domini

Dicit Dominus Jesus discipulis suis: *Ego sum via, veritas et vita; nemo venit ad Patrem nisi per me. Si* cognosceretis *me, et Patrem meum utique* cognosceretis; *et amodo cognoscetis eum et vidistis eum. Dicit ei Philippus: Domine, ostende nobis Patrem et sufficit nobis. Dicit ei Jesus: Tanto tempore vobiscum sum et non cognovistis me? Philippe, qui videt me, videt et Patrem* (Joa 14,6-9) meum. Pater *lucem* habitat *inaccessibilem* (cfr. 1 Tim 6,16), et *spiritus est Deus* (Joa 4,24), et *Deum nemo vidit unquam* (Joa 1,18). Ideo nonnisi in spiritu videri potest, quia *spiritus est qui vivificat; caro non prodest quidquam* (Joa 6,64). Sed nec filius in eo, quod aequalis est Patri, videtur ab aliquo aliter quam Pater, aliter quam Spiritus Sanctus. Unde omnes qui viderunt Dominum Jesum secundum humanitatem et non viderunt et crediderunt secundum spiritum et divinitatem, ipsum esse verum Filium Dei, damnati sunt. Ita et modo omnes qui vident sacramentum, quod sanctificatur per verba Domini super altare per manum sacerdotis in forma panis et vini, et non vident et credunt secundum spiritum et divinitatem, quod sit veraciter sanctissimum corpus et sanguis Domini nostri Jesu Christi, damnati sunt, ipso Altissimo attestante, qui ait: *Hoc est corpus meum* et *sanguis* mei *novi testamenti* [*qui pro multis effundetur*] (cfr. Mc 14,22.24); et: *Qui manducat* carnem meam *et bibit* sanguinem meum, *habet vitam aeternam* (cfr. Joa 6,55). Unde spiritus Domini, qui habitat in

1

fidelibus suis, ille est qui recipit sanctissimum corpus et sanguinem Domini. Omnes alii, qui non habent de eodem spiritu et praesumunt recipere eum, *iudicium sibi* manducant *et* bibunt (cfr. 1 Cor 11,29).

Unde: *Filii hominum, usquequo gravi corde?* (Ps 4,3). Ut quid non cognoscitis veritatem et creditis *in Filium Dei* (cfr. Joa 9,35)? Ecce, quotidie humiliat se (cfr. Phil 2,8), sicut quando *a regalibus sedibus* (Sap 18,15) venit in uterum Virginis; quotidie venit ad nos ipse humilis apparens; quotidie descendit de *sinu Patris* (cfr. Joa 1,18) super altare in manibus sacerdotis. Et sicut sanctis apostolis in vera carne, ita et modo se nobis ostendit in sacro pane. Et sicut ipsi intuitu carnis suae tantum eius carnem videbant, sed ipsum Deum esse credebant oculis spiritualibus contemplantes, sic et nos videntes panem et vinum oculis corporeis videamus et credamus firmiter, eius sanctissimum corpus et sanguinem vivum esse et verum. Et tali modo semper est Dominus cum fidelibus suis, sicut ipse dicit: *Ecce ego vobiscum sum usque ad consummationem saeculi* (cfr. Mt 28,20).

Concerning the Body of the Lord

The Lord Jesus said to his disciples: *"I am the way, the truth, and the life. No one comes to the Father, but through me. If you had known me, you would have also known my father. And from this time forth you do know Him and you have seen Him."*

2

Philip said to Him, "Lord, show us the father and it is enough for us."Jesus said to him, "Have I been so long a time with you, and you have not known me? Philip, he who sees me, sees also my Father. (John 14:6-9) *The Father abides in light inaccessible* (1 Timothy 6:16). *God is spirit* (John 4:24). *No one ever sees God* (John 1:18). For that reason, He can only be seen in the Spirit, because *the spirit gives life; the flesh does not profit anything* (John 6:64). But in truth, the Son is the equal of the Father. He too can be seen only in the way we see the Father and the Holy Spirit. In this way, all persons are damned who saw the Lord Jesus in his humanity and did not see or believe in spirit his divinity, that he was the true Son of God. Therefore, in this way, all persons are damned who see the sacrament which is made holy through the word of the Lord, lifted above the altar by the hands of the priest, in the form of bread and wine, and do not see or believe in spirit his divinity, that this is truly the most holy Body and Blood of the Lord, Jesus Christ. The Most High Himself attests, who said, *"This is my Body and my Blood of the New Covenant [which is shed on behalf of many]"* (Mark 14:22-23) and *"Who eats my flesh and drinks my blood has life everlasting."* (John 6:55). It is the Spirit of the Lord, who lives in his faithful, those who accept the most holy body and blood of the Lord. All others, who do not have the Spirit and presume to receive this, eat and drink *judgment to themselves* (1 Corinthians 11:29).

O Son of man, how long will you be dull of heart? (Psalm 4:3) Why do you refuse to recognize the truth *and believe the Son of God?* (John 9:35) Behold, day by day *He humbles himself (*Phil 2:8) just as He came from his *royal throne* (Wisdom 18:15) into the Virgin's womb. Daily, He comes to us and appears humble. Daily, he descends from the *bosom of his father* (John 1:18) into the hands of the priest at the high altar. And just as He showed himself to His holy apostles in true flesh, He shows himself to us in sacred bread. And just as they themselves saw only His flesh, but they believed Him to be God as they regarded Him with spiritual eyes. So we see with the eyes of our bodies only bread and wine, and believing steadfastly the very same to be the most holy body and blood, living and true. And in this way, the Lord is always with his faithful friends, as he said, *"Behold, I shall always be with you, even to the end of time."* (Matthew 28:20)

Reflection Concerning the Body of the Lord

Francis' words in this first of the admonitions are grounded in a thoroughly orthodox understanding of the Eucharist. Jesus is truly present with us, body and blood, soul and divinity, in the sacrament of the Eucharist. As St. Paul warned the Christians of Corinth, eating and drinking the sacrament of the altar without recognizing the Lord in the sacrament is hazardous to our spiritual, and even physical, health.

It's significant for any reflection on Franciscan spirituality that the very first thing Francis had to say to the brothers was to remind them of the importance of recognizing the Lord Jesus in the sacrament of the Eucharist. His arguments were hardly new. Each of them came from the scriptures; from First Corinthians, from the Gospel of Mark, from the Gospel of Matthew, from the Psalms, and from The Wisdom of Solomon.

The arguments distill to one very simple point. Christ, Himself, becomes present to us, under forms of consecrated bread and wine; bread and wine made holy by the praying of His own words of institution and the actions of a priest standing at the altar, offering our gifts to God and receiving back those gifts, which are changed by God's own miraculous act, in a way we can't readily either understand or physically see, into God's greatest gift to us, the gift of Himself. We must therefore, in great gratitude and love, properly receive Him.

The importance of the Eucharist to the living of the Christian life is a point that Francis made in several other of his writings. Particularly, I recall in *Letter to All the Faithful*, Francis wrote, "we all should...receive the Body and Blood of the Lord Jesus Christ. The man who does not eat His flesh and drink His blood cannot enter the kingdom of God." Also in *Letter to a General Chapter*, Francis wrote, "I beg you show the greatest reverence and honor for the most holy Body and Blood of the

Lord, Jesus Christ, through whom all things, on heaven and earth have been...reconciled with Almighty God." (Colossians 1:20) Later in that same letter, Francis wrote, "What wondrous majesty!... That the Lord of the entire universe, God, the Son of God, should humble himself like this, hiding under the form of a small bread for our salvation. See God's condescension, my brothers, and pour out your hearts before Him. (Psalm 61:9)" In *Letter to All the Superiors of the Friars Minor*, Francis wrote, "In all your sermons, you shall tell the people of the need to do penance, impressing on them that none can be saved except he receives the Body and Blood of the Lord." In *Letter to Rulers of the People*, Francis wrote, "this is my advice. Put aside all worry and anxiety. Receive the Body and Blood of the Lord Jesus Christ devoutly in memory of Him."

It is up to us to recognize, and, with a proper disposition, accept this great gift of God to us. Few things are more important in the Franciscan, indeed in the general Christian, life than for each of us to be a child of God nourished at Our Father's table so that we may be strong in the faith, strong enough in God to be able to do the work put before us.

Thank you, Father God, for providing for your children. Give us grateful hearts and willing hands, enabled to serve you.

Caput II: De malo propriae voluntatis

Dixit Dominus ad Adam: De *omni ligno comede, de ligno autem scientiae boni et mali* non *comedas* (cfr. Gen 2,16.17). De omni ligno paradisi poterat comedere, quia, dum non venit contra obedientiam, non peccavit. Ille enim comedit de ligno scientiae boni, qui sibi suam voluntatem appropriat et se exaltat de bonis, quae Dominus dicit et operatur in ipso; et sic per suggestionem diaboli et transgressionem mandati factum est pomum scientiae mali. Unde oportet, quod sustineat poenam.

On the evil of self-will

The Lord said to Adam, "From all the trees you may eat, however, you may not eat from the tree of the knowledge of good and evil." (Genesis 2:16-17) He (Adam) was able to eat from all the trees of paradise, and while he did not disobey, he did not sin. That man indeed eats of the tree of the knowledge of good who appropriates to himself his own will and praises himself concerning the good which the Lord says and works in him. Even so, in this way, through the suggestion of the Devil and the violation of the commandment, the fruit is made the knowledge of evil. From there, it is necessary he endures the penalty.

Reflection on the evil of self-will

We live in an age where it is common for people to take credit for good things they didn't do. Perhaps, it's always been so.

Certainly, it was enough of a problem in Francis' day that he had to speak up about this, particularly as the brothers were claiming credit for the good works God was doing in them as though they themselves were entirely responsible for their advances in virtue.

In Celano's *Second Life of St. Francis*, Chapter 97, there are retold Francis' own words against people who praised themselves: "No one should boast of himself with evil praise over what a sinner is able to accomplish. A sinner can fast, pray, and mortify his body. What he cannot do is to be faithful to the Lord. Therefore, this is what we should glory in, that we give glory to God, that we serve Him faithfully, that we ascribe to Him whatever He has given to us."

In *The Legend of Perugia*, 104, we're shown Francis saying: "An artist, painting a portrait of our Lord or the Blessed Virgin does them honor and recalls them to our minds. However, the painting is nothing more than what it is, something made of wood and color. The servant of God is like that painting; a creation of God through whom God is honored because of His blessings. He (God's servant) must not claim any more merit than the wood and color do. Honor and glory must be given only to God."

In the sixth chapter of *Major Life of St. Francis*, Bonaventure wrote Francis said, "A man is who he is before God and no more." This is a common theme in Francis' teachings. We will see it over and over again as we walk through the admonitions, as this emphasis on unflinching self-knowledge, penitence, and matter-of-fact soul deep humility is very much a part of what it is to be a Franciscan.

May God allow us always to give Him the credit for all the good gifts He has given us!

Caput III: De perfecta obedientia

Dicit Dominus in Evangelio: *Qui non* renuntiaverit *omnibus, quae possidet, non potest meus esse discipulus* (Lc 14,33); et: *Qui voluerit animam suam salvam facere perdet illam* (Lc 9,24). Ille homo relinquit omnia, quae possidet, et perdit corpus suum, qui se ipsum totum praebet ad obedientiam in manibus sui praelati. Et quidquid facit et dicit, quod ipse sciat, quod non sit contra voluntatem eius, dum bonum sit quod facit, vera obedientia est. Et si quando subditus videat meliora et utiliora animae suae quam ea, quae sibi praelatus praecipiat, sua voluntarie Deo sacrificet; quae autem sunt praelati, opere studeat adimplere. Nam haec est caritativa obedientia (cfr. 1 Petr 1,22), quia Deo et proximo satisfacit.

Si vero praelatus aliquid contra animam suam praecipiat, licet ei non obediat, tamen ipsum non dimittat. Et si ab aliquibus persecutionem inde sustinuerit, magis eos diligat propter Deum. Nam qui prius persecutionem sustinet, quam velit a suis fratribus separari, vere permanet in perfecta obedientia, quia ponit *animam suam* (cfr. Joa 15,13) pro fratribus suis. Sunt enim multi religiosi, qui sub specie meliora videndi quam quae sui praelati praecipiunt, retro aspiciunt (cfr. Lc 9,62) et *ad vomitum* propriae voluntatis redeunt (cfr. Prov 26,11; 2 Petr 2,22); hi homicidae sunt et propter mala sua exempla multas animas perdere faciunt.

Concerning Perfect Obedience

The Lord said in the Gospel, both "He who does not renounce all that he has cannot be my disciple" (Luke 14:33) and "He who would save his own life shall lose it" (Luke 9:24). That man relinquishes all that he has and loses himself who gives himself into the hands of his superior according to obedience. Whatever good he does and says that he knows is not contrary to the wish of his superior is true obedience. If a subordinate sees something better and more useful to his own soul than what his superior instructs, he should make a voluntary sacrifice of his own will to God while carrying out the works his superior instructs. For this is loving obedience (1 Peter 1:22) which satisfies God and neighbor.

If a superior instructs (a subordinate in) anything truly against his own conscience, he (the subordinate) cannot dismiss (the request) even though it is not proper to obey. If anyone persecutes him for this, he (the subordinate) should love him (the persecutor) all the more for the sake of God. For he who prefers to suffer rather than to be separated from his brothers, correctly continues in perfect obedience because he lays down his life (John 15:13) on behalf of his brothers. There are, in fact, many religious, who under the appearance of seeing a better way than their superior instructs, look backwards (Luke 9:62) and revert to their own will they had discharged (Proverbs 26:11; 2 Peter 2:22). These are murderers and because of their bad example they cause the loss of many souls.

Reflection concerning perfect obedience

Because of their bad example, they cause the loss of many souls; that's a harsh and all too real condemnation. Too often, people are turned away from God because of the bad example of a supposedly godly person. Sadly, our age has no unique historical claim to bad actors in the spiritual realm.

In *Rule of 1221*, Chapter 4, Francis wrote, "They (the ministers) should remember they have been entrusted with the care of the brother's souls. If any of them are lost through their (the ministers') fault or bad example, they (the ministers) must account for it before Our Lord Jesus Christ on the day of Judgment."

Bonaventure tells us in *Major Life*, Part 1, Chapter 8, "Holy Francis used to say we ought to have compassion on a preacher who sought his own glory in his work, and not the good of his listeners, or who destroyed all he had done in his teaching by the example of his bad life."

Francis, being very much a man, saw the consequences of sin and disobedience to a community. In Celano's *Second Life of St. Francis*, chapter 116, Francis says, "The best brothers are put to confusion by the actions of bad brothers. Where they themselves have not sinned, they must bear the judgment on account of the example of the wicked."

Francis found obedience to be a valid and useful tool for conquering sin. There are many references in the writings of Francis and Franciscan sources that help explain his position on obedience. A very few of those will be given next.

In *Rule of 1221*, Chapter 5, Francis wrote, "the brothers should be happy to serve and obey one another in a spirit of charity. This is the true, holy obedience, of Our Lord Jesus Christ."

In his *Letter to All the Faithful*, Francis wrote, "Our Lord says in the Gospel: 'It is from the heart of man all sin and vice comes' (Matthew 1:18-19) and He tells us, 'Love your enemies, do good to those who hate you.' (Luke 6:27) We are obligated to live our lives according to the precepts and advice of the Lord Jesus Christ. So, we renounce self and bring our lower natures into subjection under obedience. We have all promised this to God. But, no one can be coerced to obey another in anything that is either criminal or sinful."

Celano, in chapter 113 of *Second Life of St. Francis* wrote this, "Francis thought a command should only rarely be given under obedience ...However, he thought that the person who does not hurry to obey a command under obedience neither fears God nor respects man."

In Francis' poem, *Praises of the Virtues*, Francis wrote,

"Lady, holy love,
God keep you,
with your sister holy obedience.
All holy virtues, God keep you...
In all the world, there is not a man
who can possess any of you,
without first dying to himself...
Each and every one of you,
bewilders vice and sin...
Holy Obedience confounds
each physical, worldly, and selfish desire."

May God grant that in dying to ourselves we may live as more obedient children of God and come to truly show His love to our hurting world that is desperately in need of Him! ·

Caput IV: Ut nemo appropriet sibi praelationem

Non veni *ministrari, sed ministrare* (cfr. Mt 20,28), dicit Dominus. Illi qui sunt super alios constituti, tantum de illa praelatione glorientur, quantum si essent in abluendi fratrum pedes officio deputati. Et quanto magis turbantur de ablata sibi praelatione quam de pedum officio, tanto magis sibi *loculos* ad periculum animae componunt (cfr. Joa 12,6).

No one should claim the office of Superior as his own

I came not be be served, but to serve (Matthew 20:28), says the Lord. Those who are placed above others should be so much more glorified if they were deputized with the task of washing their brothers' feet than in their appointment as superior. They should be more disturbed at losing the duty of washing feet than their role as superior, so much does their place make danger to their souls.

Reflection on not claiming office

In *Rule of 1221*, chapter 6, Francis said, "No one is to be called, 'Prior.' They are all to be known as

'Lesser Brothers (Friars Minor)', with no distinction, and they should be prepared to wash each other's feet." In Chapter 17 of that same rule, Francis wrote, "The ministers must remember they do not have a right to serve the brothers...they must lay it aside without objection the moment they are instructed to do so."

In *Letter to All the Faithful*, Francis said, "The man who commands obedience and has become the greatest should be the least and serve his brothers."

In Celano's *Second Life*, Chapter 129, the perfect superior is described by Francis, saying, "He must be a man of a most serious life, of discretion and praiseworthy reputation...a man for whom zeal for prayer is a friend; a man who sets aside certain hours for his own soul and for his flock. He must start each morning with Mass and in a prolonged devotion commend himself and his flock to divine protection. Following his prayers, he should be available to all, to answer questions, to provide kindly for all. He must be a man who will not show favoritism...A man of a gift of learning who has the image of pious simplicity in his actions. A man who despises money as a cause of corruption in our profession and perfection; one who as the head of a poor order, should show himself an example for the rest, does not make a wrong use of the pocketbook. For himself, a habit and a little book should be enough, and for his brothers it is enough if he has a box of pen and a seal. He shouldn't be a collector of books...lest he

15

be taking from his duty what he gives to study. He should be a man who consoles the troubled, since he is the final recourse for the afflicted...He should move difficult people to gentleness. He should humble himself and relax his rights in order to gain a soul for Christ...I would want him to be honored...and to be provided with all that is necessary, in all charity. However, he must not take pleasure in honors...He must, finally, be a man who...will consider so great an office a burden instead of a dignity. He must not let apathy grow out of excessive kindness, nor let discipline be slack out of indulgence, so while loved by all, he will be feared by those who work evil. I wish he would have companions filled with goodness of life who will show themselves in all things an example of good works...so attractively friendly that all who come to them will be received with cheerfulness. This is what a minister general of the order should be." A similar account of Francis' assessment of the qualifications of a minister general is given in *Mirror of Perfection*, chapter 80.

Look at the description: cheerful, zealous for God, a person of prayer, caring for his/her own body and soul as well for those in his/her care, learned and pious, simple in mode of living, seeing possessions as stewardships for the glory of God. Isn't that really only what are all called to be in following Jesus, particularly following Him in the footsteps of Francis?

God, grant us always to follow Jesus in the footsteps of Francis!

Caput V: Ut nemo superbiat, sed glorietur in cruce Domini

Attende, o homo, in quanta excellentia posuerit te Dominus Deus, quia creavit et formavit te *ad imaginem* dilecti Filii sui secundum corpus *et similitudinem* (cfr. Gen 1,26) secundum spiritum. Et omnes creaturae, quae sub caelo sunt, secundum se serviunt, cognoscunt et obediunt Creatori suo melius quam tu. Et etiam daemones non crucifixerunt eum, sed tu cum ipsis crucifixisti eum et adhuc crucifigis delectando in vitiis et peccatis. Unde ergo potes gloriari? Nam si tantum esses subtilis et sapiens quod *omnem scientiam* (cfr. 1 Cor 13,2) haberes et scires interpretari omnia *genera linguarum* (cfr. 1 Cor 12,28) et subtiliter de caelestibus rebus perscrutari, in omnibus his non potes gloriari; quia unus daemon scivit de caelestibus et modo scit de terrenis plus quam omnes homines, licet aliquis fuerit, qui summae sapientiae cognitionem a Domino receperit specialem. Similiter et si esses pulchrior et ditior omnibus et etiam si faceres mirabilia, ut daemones fugares, omnia ista tibi sunt contraria et nihil ad te pertinet et in his nil potes gloriari; sed in hoc possumus gloriari *in infirmitatibus* nostris (cfr. 2 Cor 12,5) et baiulare quotidie sanctam crucem Domini nostri Jesu Christi (cfr. Lc 14,27).

In order that no one be proud, except to glory in the Cross of the Lord

Listen carefully, O man, in accordance with how great a preeminence you are placed. The Lord God created and formed you in the image of the beloved Son according to your body and in (His) likeness (Genesis 1:26) according to your spirit. All creatures which are under heaven know, serve, and obey their creator, in their own way, better than you do. Even the demons did not crucify Him, but you, with them, crucified Him, and continue to crucify Him by delighting in vice and sin.

What do you have to be proud of? For if you were so clever and wise that you knew everything (1 Corinthians 13:2), if you possessed and interpreted every kind of language (1 Cor. 12:28) and could investigate carefully, minutely, the affairs of heaven, in this you could not boast, because one demon has known more of heaven and still knows more of earthly things than all men, even one (man) who may have received a special knowledge of highest wisdom from the Lord.

Similarly, if you were the noblest and richest of all, and could do miracles such that you could put demons to flight, in all respects this is incompatible with you, and none of it pertains to you. In this, you could not boast.

But in fact, we can boast of these things; our weakness (2 Cor. 12:5) and that we daily bear the sacred cross of Our Lord, Jesus Christ (Luke 14:27).

Reflection on not being proud except in the Cross

Celano, in *First Life*, Book 2, Chapter 1, says of Francis, "For although he (Francis) was a man like ourselves, subject to the same weaknesses, he was...overflowing with the most zealous love... The passion of Jesus Christ proves this and His cross shows it with the most clarity. In truth, the venerable father was marked in five parts of his body with the emblems of the passion and the cross as if he had hung upon the cross with the Son of God."

Few of us will ever be as united to Christ in His passion as Francis was. Few of us would even want to become, as Francis came to be, a living crucifix, bearing in our body the wounds of Christ's crucifixion. Yet, Francis did endure the pain of these sacred wounds. And even in this intense state of union, Francis was humble, hiding the stigmata as best he could, letting few people see the wounds, keeping this gift of God to himself, guarding it, treasuring it, even as the Blessed Mother kept, pondered, and treasured in her heart all the things told her by Gabriel, the shepherds, the Magi, and Simeon and Anna in the Temple.

No one knows if this admonition was given before or after Francis received the stigmata. Either way, it really doesn't matter. Our Blessed Lord Himself did tell us, as recorded in chapter 14 of Luke's Gospel, that no one could be His disciple who was unwilling to take up his/her cross and follow Him.

It is good counsel that we have large cause for humility. I recall Isaiah 64:6, "We all have become as one unclean, and all our righteous acts are as a menstruating woman's rag." That's harsh, and more graphic than we likely want to contemplate. But it is all too fitting to describe our state and the true worth of even our most just actions. We who were made in the image of God fail so often in being true servants of God and have nothing at all to brag about, except our weaknesses and that we can, and God willing do, choose to unite ourselves to Christ in his passion.

In *Rule of 1221*, Chapter 17, Francis said, "We must be on our guard against pride and empty boasting." Pride and empty boasting were both well known to Francis prior to his conversion. Celano, in chapter one of *First Life of St. Francis*, is clear on this: "Francis was from his earliest years brought up by his parents to be proud of spirit."

Yet, Francis' public ministry is distinguished by his deep humility and utter dependence on God. He'd known pride intimately and had repented of it. Knowing the danger of pride, he was always on guard against it. Bonaventure, in *Major Life*, Part 1, Chapter 6, tells us, "The saint had a horror of pride which is the cause of all evil and of disobedience which is its worst offspring."

In Part 1, Chapter 8, of *Major Life*, Bonaventure recounts that St. Francis, while praying about the bad example some of the inexperienced brothers had given, when Jesus spoke to him, "Poor man, what are you worried about? When I made you the shepherd of my order, do you think I stopped being its first protector? The true reason I chose you was because you had nothing to boast about. What I do in you will be attributed to divine grace, not to the actions of men."

Bonaventure told us a good deal about Francis' love for the Cross of Christ. In Part 2, Chapter 1 of *Major Life*, Bonaventure tells us, "All Francis' efforts, whether known to others or made in secret, were aimed towards the cross of Our Lord." In Part 1, Chapter 9, of *Major Life*, Bonaventure wrote, "The memory of Jesus Christ crucified was always in his heart like a bundle of myrrh."

I love that particular imagery Bonaventure used. Myrrh, unlike other plant resins burned for incense, does not melt under heat, rather it "blooms" or expands when heat is applied. I can almost see the memory of Christ Crucified blooming in Francis' heart under the fire of divine love. At times in history, myrrh has been more valuable than gold. Certainly, for Francis, this symbolic bundle of myrrh in his heart, the memory of the Crucified, was far more valuable than all the gold in the world.

May God grant us the grace that we may always hold the memory of Christ Jesus, Crucified, Resurrected, Glorified, as our most valuable possession!

Caput VI: De imitatione Domini

Attendamus, omnes fratres, bonum pastorem, qui pro ovibus suis salvandis crucis sustinuit passionem. Oves Domini secutae fuerunt eum in tribulatione et persecutione, verecundia et fame, in infirmitate et tentatione et ceteris aliis; et de his receperunt a Domino vitam sempiternam. Unde magna verecundia est nobis servis Dei, quod sancti fecerunt opera et nos recitando ea volumus recipere gloriam et honorem.

Concerning the imitation of the Lord

Let us all listen carefully, brothers, the Good Shepherd bore the passion of the cross in order to save his sheep. The Lord's sheep followed him in trials, persecutions, and shame, in hunger and thirst, in weakness and temptation, and in all the rest. And from this, they have received eternal life from the Lord. Wherefore, it is an intense shame for us, the servants of God, that where the Saints have done works, we read aloud the same and wish to receive honor and glory.

Reflection concerning the imitation of the Lord

Francis' respect for the saints is seen nowhere more clearly than in Chapter 23 of *Rule of 1221* where he prays to the Father, "We are poor sinners, unworthy to mention your name, so we beg...his glorious mother Mary...Saint John the Baptist, John the Evangelist, Saints Peter and Paul, all the holy Patriarchs, Prophets, Innocents, Apostles, Evangelists, Martyrs, Confessors, Virgins...and all the other saints, living and dead or still to come, we beg them all most humbly, for the love of you, to give thanks to you, the most high, eternal God, living and true."

Francis, in his *Office of the Passion*, wrote this antiphon to Mary:

"Holy Virgin Mary, there is no one like you born on earth among women: You are the daughter and the handmaid of the Most High King and Father of Heaven; You are the mother of our most holy Lord, Jesus Christ; You are the spouse of the Holy Spirit. With Saint Michael the Archangel, all the Virtues of Heaven, and all the Saints, pray for us before your most holy, beloved, Son, Lord, and Master."

Bonaventure wrote in *Major Life*, Part 1, Chapter 9, "He (Francis) embraced the Mother of Our Lord Jesus with inexpressible love because, he said, it was she who made the Lord of Majesty our brother, and through her we found mercy. After Christ, he put all his trust in her and took her as his patroness, for himself and his brothers... He had an unmovable love for the Angels who burn with a marvelous fire, such that they are in ecstasy to God and desire to inflame the souls of the chosen...In his ardent zeal for the salvation of souls, he (Francis) was especially devoted to Saint Michael the Archangel, because it is his (Michael's) task to bring souls before God. The mercy of all the saints, who are burning coals in God's temple, kindled in Francis a divine fire such that he embraced all the Apostles with the greatest of affection, especially Saints Peter and Paul on account of their passionate love for Christ...Christ's beggar, Francis, had only two mites which he could generously give in charity, his body and his soul. However, in his love for Christ, he (Francis) spent those without ceasing so that he seemed to always be burning up his body by fasting or his soul by ardent desire (for closeness with God). In this manner, he (Francis) offered a visible burnt sacrifice like the priests in the court of the temple while burning sweet-smelling herbs on the altar of his heart."

In *The Legend of Perugia*, Chapter 70, we read that Francis said, "We see many people today who would like to take honor and glory to themselves by being content with singing about the exploits of others."

In Chapter 74 of that same work, we see Francis saying, "The worth of knowledge is proportional to the actions it produces. There is no better sermon than the practice of the virtues."

And that's the point of this admonition, the Christian life, particularly the Franciscan life, is not a spectator's sport. It is not enough to know and love God and to develop a friendship with His holy angels and His saints. It's not enough to just talk about God and the great actions of those who have gone before us in their pilgrimage of faith. We, like Francis, really only have two things we can ever generously give to God—our bodies and our souls. And we must give Him both to walk with Him.

May God grant us always to be willing to give both our bodies and souls to Him generously, not sparing ourselves, for His glory and honor!

Caput VII: Ut bona operatio sequatur scientiam

Dicit apostolus: *Littera occidit, spiritus autem vivificat* (2 Cor 3,6). Illi sunt mortui a littera, qui tantum sola verba cupiunt scire, ut sapientiores teneantur inter alios et possint acquirere magnas divitias dantes consanguineis et amicis. Et illi religiosi sunt mortui a littera, qui spiritum divinae litterae nolunt sequi, sed solum verba magis cupiunt scire et aliis interpretari. Et illi sunt vivificati a spiritu divinae litterae, qui omnem litteram, quam sciunt et cupiunt scire, non attribuunt corpori, sed verbo et exemplo reddunt ea altissimo Domino Deo, cuius est omne bonum.

Good works must follow knowledge

The Apostle said: "The letter kills, however the Spirit gives life." (2 Corinthians 3:6) Those are killed by the letter who only wish to know so much of the Word in order that they may be thought wise among others and to acquire great wealth to give to their family and friends. Those religious are killed by the letter who will not follow the spirit of the Holy Scriptures, but only desire to know so much of the Word to explain to others. Those are made alive by the spirit of Holy Scriptures who do not attribute to self all the letters they know or desire to know, but who by word and example return them to the Almighty Lord God, of whom is every good.

Reflection on good works following knowledge

Celano, in *First Life*, Book 1, Chapter 9, wrote about Francis, "For he wasn't a deaf hearer of the Gospel, but committing all he heard to memory, he strove diligently to carry it out."

In *Second Life*, Chapter 68, Celano wrote of Francis, "he had a deep understanding of the Scriptures...At times, he would read the holy books and what he placed once in his mind, he wrote permanently in his heart. His memory substituted for books, because he didn't once hear a thing in vain. His love meditated on it with constant devotion. This, he would say, was a profitable way of studying and reading...The man who put nothing before his desire for eternal life, he (Francis) considered a true philosopher. He often said a man who would study the Scriptures humbly, not presumptuously, would move more easily from knowledge of himself to knowledge of God."

In *Major Life*, Part 1, Chapter 11, Bonaventure wrote of Francis, "Once he had read something in the holy books, and understood its meaning, he impressed it indelibly upon his memory. Anything he had once carefully grasped, he meditated on constantly. When the brothers asked him if he would allow the scholars who were entering the Order to continue to study Sacred Scripture, he (Francis) replied, 'Provided they don't neglect prayer, after the example of Christ, who prayed more than he studied, I don't mind. They shouldn't study just to have something to say. They should study in order to practice what they have learned and to encourage others to do the same. I want my brothers to be true disciples of the Gospel and to grow in knowledge of truth, growing in simplicity without separating the simplicity of the dove from the cunning of the snake, because Our Lord Himself joined them in one phrase.'"

While we don't know for a fact that St. Francis actually wrote the *Letter to Saint Anthony*, the text of that letter is in agreement with the rest of what we've just seen, in that it says, "That you should teach the brothers theology is acceptable to me provided they (the brothers) do not extinguish the spirit of prayer and devotion, as given in the Rule, because of this study."

In *Second Life*, Chapter 71, Celano relays the encounter between Francis and a brother. The brother encouraged Francis to take comfort by reading scripture. Francis replied, "It is good to read the testimony of scripture. It is good to seek Our Lord God in them. I now truly have so much of the Scripture that I have more than enough to contemplate... By no means do I require more, son. I know Christ, the poor Crucified (1 Corinthians 2:2)."

For Francis, nothing was more important than to continually live in a spirit of prayer and devotion to God, to be in friendship with Jesus. In *Letter to All the Faithful*, Francis wrote, "But, in fact, O how much they are blessed and happy who love God and do as the Lord himself said in the Gospel, 'You shall love the Lord your God from your entire heart and from your whole mind and your neighbor as yourself' (Matthew 22: 37 and 39). Therefore, we must love God and worship Him with a pure heart and a clean mind because this is what He demands above all things, saying 'Real worshippers adore the Father in spirit and in truth. All, in fact, who worship him, it is necessary to worship in the spirit of truth' (John 4:23-24). Also we should devote praise and prayer to Him, day and night, saying, 'Our Father who art in heaven' (Matthew 6:9), because it is proper we should always pray and not fail."

Over and over again, Francis brings home his desire that the purpose of study— whether that is of the Scriptures or of Theology, or of any other subject matter—is to equip us for living out the life of a disciple of Jesus Christ, for doing the work the

Lord has for us to do, not for building ourselves up in pride because of anything we may accomplish through study.

Francis knew the real dangers of study and wished his brothers and sisters to avoid those as much as possible. The first danger is that we may come to study more than we pray, which is in direct opposition to the example set by Jesus and, indeed, is deadly to our souls. The second is that we would come to take pride in our intellectual achievements, instead of recognizing that anything good that we do is only because the Lord has done it through us.

May all of us always be considered by Francis to be true philosophers, having put nothing ahead of eternity!

Caput VIII: De peccato invidiae vitando

Ait apostolus: *Nemo potest dicere: Dominus Jesus, nisi in Spiritu Sancto* (1 Cor 12,3); et: *Non est qui faciat bonum, non est usque ad unum* (Rom 3,12). Quicumque ergo invidet fratri suo de bono, quod Dominus dicit et facit in ipso, pertinet ad peccatum blasphemiae, quia ipsi Altissimo invidet (cfr. Mt 20,15), qui dicit et facit omne bonum.

Concerning avoiding the sin of envy

The Apostle asserts: "No one is able to say 'Jesus is Lord' except in the Holy Spirit" (1 Corinthians 12:3) and 'There is none who does good, not one" (Romans 3:12). Whoever envies his brother concerning his good, which the Lord has said and done in him, commits the sin of blasphemy because he envies the Most High himself, who says and does all good.

Reflection on avoiding envy

Envy as blasphemy? It's quite a thing to ponder, now, isn't it? I'd never seen it phrased that powerfully, until the first time I'd read the *Admonitions*.

These words of Francis had the same impact on my soul as the 15th chapter of 1st Samuel— where rebellion was equated to witchcraft and disobedience to idolatry— did the first time I read that passage from 1st Samuel during my teenage years. Both passages robbed me of breath and brought me, immediately, to repentance.

But my own personal reflections aside, the last phrase of this admonition reminds me forcibly of the prayer that ends St. Francis' *Laudes ad Omnes Horas Dicendae* (Praises Near Each Appointed Hour, literally translated), commonly called in English, *The Praises before the Office*. Because the Latin is so quintessentially Francis, I'll go ahead and give this to you in the Latin, then translate it for you.

Omnipotens sanctissime, altissime et summe Deus, omne bonum, summum bonum, totum bonum, qui solus es bonus (cfr. Lc 18,19), tibi reddamus omnem laudem, omnem gloriam, omnem gratiam, omnem honorem, omnem benedictionem et omnia bona. Fiat. Fiat. Amen.

All powerful, most sacred, highest and greatest God, all good, the highest good, complete good, who alone is good (Luke 18:19), to you we render all praise, all glory, all gratitude, all honor, all blessing, and every good. It is being done. It is being done. So be it.

Towards the end of *Rule of 1221*, Francis wrote words that also remind me of this last clause in the *Admonition*, besides being good advice for our spiritual priorities: "We should desire and wish for nothing else, we should take no pleasures or delight in anything else except in our Creator, Redeemer, and Savior. He alone is true God, who is full good, true and complete good, who alone is good (Luke 18:19), faithful, gentle, agreeable, and sweet, who alone is kind, upright, pure, and from Him, through Him, and in Him is all pardon, all grace, and all glory for the penitent, the just, and the blessed in heaven who rejoice together."

May we always rejoice in the good that the Lord has done for us. But more importantly let us continually rejoice in the good He does for those around us, seeing God's hand at work in all things and all people, while rejoicing with the Saints over the goodness of the Lord!

Caput IX: De dilectione

Dicit Dominus: *Diligite inimicos vestros* [*benefacite his qui oderunt vos, et orate pro persequentibus et calumniantibus vos*] (Mt 5,44). Ille enim veraciter diligit inimicum suum, qui non dolet de iniuria, quam sibi facit, sed de peccato animae suae uritur propter amorem Dei. Et ostendat ei ex operibus dilectionem.

Concerning Love

The Lord said: "Love your enemies [be good to those who hate you, and pray for those who persecute and falsely accuse you] (Matthew 5:44). Indeed, that person truly loves his foe who does not grieve in respect to an injury done to himself, but burns on account of the love of God about the sin of their (the foes') souls, and shows that love from works.

Reflection concerning Love

In *Rule of 1221*, Chapter 11, Francis wrote to his brothers, "And by no means become angry, 'Everyone who is angry with his brother is liable to judgment; and whoever says to his brother, "Raca", shall be liable to the Sanhedrin; and whoever says, "You fool!" shall be liable to the fire of Gehenna

(Matthew 5:22)...And they shall show their love by works...as the apostle says, 'Let us not love in word, neither with the tongue, but in works and truth. (1 John 3:18)"

Judaism teaches that to cause a person to blush with shame or embarrassment is the same as shedding his/her blood in violence. That's why denouncing someone as 'raca', literally in Aramaic as an empty head, would place one at the mercy of the Sanhedrin or why calling someone 'fool' would earn the caller Hellfire or Gehenna. That embarrassment resulting from the name calling, in Jewish teaching, would be the same as inflicting bodily injury or even committing murder, depending on the intensity of the embarrassment caused. Jesus knew that, when he gave the Sermon on the Mount from which this quotation from Matthew comes.

In *Letter to a Minister*, Francis wrote: "I say to you, as you can, with regard to the function of your soul, consider anything that hinders you to love the Lord God (to be) a grace, whether that hindrance is made by the brothers or anyone else, even if they strike you. And thus by no means should you wish it changed. This is to you by means of obedience to the Lord God and to me because I steadfastly know that this is true obedience. You must love those who do this to you. And you should not want different from them, except what the Lord gives to you. Even in the midst of this, love them and be willing that they should be better Christians."

That's no easier to live with than the original advice. Too often, when faced with difficult and hurtful people, our first inclination is to invoke a slightly modified blessing for the Czar from the musical *Fiddler on the Roof:* "Lord bless and keep (insert name)...far away from us!" Yet, not only does Francis require that we rejoice for, and not envy, people for the good things God has given them, he requires we understand the difficulties people make for us are part of God's good gifts, given to us for our good, as well.

All of this way of reacting to injuries done to us by others is contrary to the fallen nature of human beings. None of this love for others is possible unless we live always in a constant friendship with our Lord. I have a button, somewhere, that says, "God's grace makes things possible, not easy!"

May God grant us the grace to always see God's hand in all things, in all actions of people around us, whether those are pleasant or challenging!

Caput X: De castigatione corporis

Multi sunt, qui dum peccant vel iniuriam recipiunt, saepe inculpant inimicum vel proximum. Sed non est ita: quia unusquisque in sua potestate habet inimicum, videlicet corpus, per quod peccat. Unde *beatus ille servus* (Mt 24,46), qui talem inimicum traditum in sua potestate semper captum tenuerit et sapienter se ab ipso custodierit; quia dum hoc fecerit, nullus alius inimicus visibilis vel invisibilis ei nocere poterit.

Concerning the reproof of self

There are many who while they experience sin or injury, often blame (their) enemy or neighbor. But this is not so. Each one has his enemy in his own power, clearly the body through which he sins. Blessed that servant (Matthew 24:46) who always holds captive that enemy in his power and wisely guards himself from it, because while this is done, no other enemy, visible or invisible, is able to do harm to him.

Reflection on the reproving one's self

It's been part of the human condition to blame others for our own sins, all the way back to the Fall when Adam blamed Eve and Eve blamed the Serpent. In addition to blaming others, we are all too often our own worst enemy. And yet, Francis called for each of us to take responsibility for ourselves, for our own acts.

Further, he calls us to take preemptive action to conquer self, just to get ourselves out of the way and under control, so that we cannot be harmed by any other enemy, whether in the physical or spiritual realms. That's a big task Francis sets before us; one that we couldn't even begin to undertake if we had not committed to live our lives in the following of Jesus. We need the graces that come from staying close to Jesus in order to be able to do this.

In Celano's *Second Life,* Chapter 133, Francis speaks of the good that comes from temptation, "In truth, no one should consider himself a servant of God (Acts 16:17) until he has gone through temptations and troubles (Judith 8:22-23). In a certain way, conquered temptation is a ring with which the Lord betroths the soul of His servant to Himself. There are many who are flattered in themselves concerning their old merits and are delighted that they do not undergo temptation. In fact, since fear would destroy them before the battle, they should know their own soul's weakness has been considered by the Lord. That is, fierce struggles are scarcely present except where strength has been accomplished."

May the Lord give us always His good and perfect gifts, and the strength to live joyfully with those blessings.

Caput XI: Ut nemo corrumpatur malo alterius

Servo Dei nulla res displicere debet praeter peccatum. Et quocumque modo aliqua persona peccaret, et propter hoc servus Dei non ex caritate turbaretur et irasceretur, thesaurizat sibi culpam (cfr. Rom 2,5). Ille servus Dei, qui non irascitur neque conturbat se pro aliquo recte vivit sine proprio. Et beatus est, qui non remanet sibi aliquid reddens *quae sunt caesaris caesari, et quae sunt Dei Deo* (Mt 22,21).

In order that no one be damaged by another's sins

To the servant of God, nothing should be displeasing except sin. No matter which way another sins, the servant of God should not be disturbed or angry, except out of charity because he gathers a treasure of blame to himself (Romans 2:5). That servant of God who is not angered or disquieted by anything, on his own behalf, lives correctly without property. He is blessed who keeps nothing for himself, but renders *to Caesar that which are Caesar's, and to God that which are God's.* (Matthew 22:21)

Reflection on not being damaged by other's sins

In *Rule of 1221*, Chapter 5, Francis wrote, "All the brothers, the ministers who are servants and the others, should take precautions not to be disturbed or angered by the sins or bad (actions) of others. The devil wishes to corrupt many on account of the fault of one. However, spiritually, as best they can, they (the brothers) help that one who sins. It is not the healthy who need a doctor, but the sick. (Matthew 9:12, Mark 2:17)"

In *Letter to a Minister,* Francis wrote, "In this regard, I wish to learn if you love God and me, His servant and yours. There must be no brother in the world who sins, to whatever degree he is able to sin, who after looking in your eyes, withdraws without your pity if he seeks mercy. And if he doesn't ask for mercy, you should demand after the very same, if he wishes mercy. And if he comes before your eyes a thousand times afterwards, you should love him more than me, in order that you may draw him to the Lord. You must always show so great mercy."

It would be easy to skip over the part that says, *The servant of God who is not angered or disquieted by anything, on his own behalf, lives correctly without property.* "Without property" is given in the Latin as "sine proprio". Literally, that's "without (one's) own". However, in ecclesiastical Latin, that is nearly always rendered as "without property" and it's a term given for living a life of voluntary poverty. Skipping over this sentence in the *Admonitions* and the sentence that immediately follows it would be a vast disservice to understanding what Francis was truly getting at in this admonition.

In *Legend of the Three Companions,* Chapter 8, the story is told of how Francis, with his initial companions, went into a church, prayed for guidance, asking God to show them the way they should live. Kneeling before the altar, praying that God would show them His will, Francis opened the

Book of the Gospels to Matthew 19:21, "If you would be perfect, go, sell all that you have, and give it to the poor, and you will have treasure in heaven." Francis thanked God with great joy for this guidance, then because he was devoted to the Trinity, he wanted a threefold confirmation of this instruction. He closed and reopened the Gospels a second and third time, revealing the passage from Luke 9:3 and Matthew 16:24 respectively. Namely, "Take nothing for your journey" and "If any man would follow me, let him deny himself." At this point, Francis declared this was both their rule and their life, instructing them to go and do as they'd heard from the Gospel readings.

If the Franciscan life were a building, then the foundation would be voluntary poverty undertaken for the love of God. In part 1, chapter 7 of *Major Life,* Bonaventure wrote, "He (Francis) used to say this (poverty) was the foundation that the Order in such a way that it (poverty) was the primary under-layment for the entire structure of the Order; that if it (poverty) were strong the Order would stand, but if it were weakened the Order would utterly collapse."

Also in that same chapter of *Major Life*, Bonaventure says of Francis, "The brothers, in conclave, asked him (Francis) what virtue rendered one more friendly to Christ. He replied, as though revealing his deepest secret, 'You must know, Brothers, poverty is a special way of salvation just as if it were the kindling of humility and the root of perfection. Its fruit is numerous but hidden. This is the treasure hidden in the field (Matthew 13:44) of the Gospel. To buy it, we must sell all."

Francis continued later in that same chapter, "By no means has he perfectly renounced the world who holds on to his own opinions in the secret places of his heart."

This last statement of Francis is reinforced in Celano's *Second Life,* chapter 102, "Through revelation, he (Francis) had learned understanding about many things, yet in conversation he would place the thoughts of others above (his own). He believed the counsel of his companions to be safer and the vision of another seemed better than his own. He (Francis) used to say that one has not given up all things for the Lord (Matthew 19:27) who has retained the money-box of his own opinions."

Most Franciscans do not live our lives under the evangelical councils; we don't take vows of poverty, chastity, and obedience. Yet, all Franciscans seek to live our lives, as best we can in our circumstances, within the Franciscan Charism. When Francis formed the Brothers and Sisters of Penitence (or Brothers and Sisters of Continence, as both names are used in various documents), the Third Order of St. Francis, it was to let those of us in the world, who were unable to enter traditional religious communities, live our lives intentionally, for the glory of God, for the health of our souls, and most of all for the good of others, in the Franciscan way.

If Jesus is the Lord of our lives, then all that we are, all that we have, must be surrendered to God.

Everything we have, even our opinions, belongs properly to God. For us to retain control of anything is to fail to render to God the things that are God's.

There's a good deal to think about in these few words. We are not to be bothered by anything except sin. Even then, if our anger at a sin is motivated by anything except love for the sinner, we're sinning ourselves because we're refusing to give everything we possess over to God in that we're holding onto our own opinions in the secret places of our hearts.

May God grant us all the grace to allow Him to truly be the Lord of our lives, to give Him control of every aspect of our lives and to keep nothing, not even our own opinions in those secret places in our hearts, under our own control!

Caput XII:De cognoscendo spiritu Domini

Sic potest cognosci servus Dei, si habet de spiritu Domini: cum Dominus operaretur per ipsum aliquod bonum, si caro eius non inde se exaltaret, quia semper est contraria omni bono, sed si magis ante oculos se haberet viliorem et omnibus aliis hominibus minorem se existimaret.

Concerning Recognizing the Lord's Spirit

This is how the servant of the Lord can learn if he has the spirit of the Lord: when the Lord has worked anything good though the person, if his low passion, which is ever contrary to all good, is not exalted, but instead, in his own eyes, he esteems himself more vile and smaller than all other men.

Reflection on recognizing the Lord's Spirit

Have you ever found yourself feeling proud of being humble?

Humility is one of the hardest of the virtues for modern man. We don't do it very well. Besides, we tend not to see humility as a virtue but instead as a defect in character, a weakness. Humble people are seen, in our age, as doormats. Yet, nothing could be further from the truth.

Still, I suspect that attitude wasn't really much different in Francis' time. The trappings of human life have changed dramatically in the last few centuries. But the human heart hasn't changed since the Fall.

In chapter 17 of *Rule of 1221,* Francis wrote, "The Spirit of God, however, wishes us to subdue and despise and humble the vile self. The Spirit desires humility, patience, purity, simplicity, and true peace. Always, above all, He (the Spirit) desires the fear of God, the wisdom of God, and the divine love of the Father, Son, and Holy Spirit."

Francis taught humility more in his example than in his words. Celano in *Second Life*, chapter 102, wrote of Francis, "Humility is the guardian and elegance of all the virtues...Forgetting what he (Francis) had gained, he set before his eyes only his shortcomings, considering himself to lack more than he gained. His only ambition was to grow strong so that he could become better; not content with the first, he sought to add new virtues...This prince of God was not known as a superior except because of this gleaming gem that among the 'Lesser' he was the least. This virtue, this title, this insignia showed he was the minister general."

In chapter 103, Celano continues his description of Francis' humility, describing an incident in which Francis, quite ill, rode a donkey through the field of a peasant. The peasant man came up to them, asking if this was Francis. When Francis acknowledged he was indeed himself, the peasant admonished Francis not to let his followers down, to always show himself to be the good and holy man whom people believed him to be. Then Francis, even though he was unable to walk any distance, being ill and weak, climbed down off the donkey and prostrated himself at the feet of the peasant farmer, kissing the peasant's feet in love, and thanking him for his kindness in encouraging him. That's the background for the following statement of Celano about Francis, "Therefore, he was so honored and famous to be just as a saint to many, he considered himself worthless in the presence of God and man."

In *Mirror of Perfection*, Chapter 72, Francis is said to have taught the brothers to build their lives on humility, pure simplicity, devout prayer, the love of Lady Poverty, saying this was the only sure way to our own salvation and the building up of others, citing that Jesus showed and taught us this way by His words and the example of His holy life.

And that's what the Franciscan life is about, following Jesus, living our lives in discipleship.

God grant us to grow in humility so that we may more easily confess "We are only unprofitable servants", especially after we've done great things!

Caput XIII: De patientia

Non potest cognoscere servus Dei, quantam habeat patientiam et humilitatem in se, dum satisfactum est sibi. Cum autem venerit tempus, quod illi qui deberent sibi satisfacere, faciunt sibi contrarium, quantam ibi patientiam et humilitatem tantam habet et non plus.

Concerning patience

The servant of God is not able to learn how much

patience and humility he possesses in himself while he himself is satisfied. However, when the time will come that those who ought to satisfy him act in contradiction to him, he has then that much patience and humility and no more.

Reflection concerning patience

Francis dictated *Concerning True and Perfect Joy* to Brother Leo. It's perhaps the best example of what Francis is speaking of in this *Admonition*. The text of that short work follows:

One day at St. Mary's, St Francis called Brother Leo and said: "Brother Leo, write this down."

He (Br. Leo) answered, "Look! I'm ready."

"Write what true joy is," he (Francis) said. "A messenger comes and says that all the masters of theology in Paris have joined the Order — write that is not true joy. Or all the prelates beyond the mountain — archbishops and bishops, or the King of France and the King of England — write that is not true joy. Or that my friars have gone to the infidels and have converted all of them to the faith; or that I have so much grace from God that I heal the sick and I perform many miracles. I tell you that true joy is not in all those things."

"But what is true joy?"

"I am returning from Perugia and I am coming here at night, in the dark. It is winter time and wet and muddy and so cold that icicles form at the edges of my habit and keep striking my legs, and blood flows from such wounds. And I come to the gate, all covered with mud and cold and ice, and after I have knocked and called for a long time, a friar comes and demands 'Who are you?' I answer 'Brother Francis.' And he says 'Go away. This is not a decent hour. You will not enter.'

"And I, for a second time, press on. He replies, 'Go away. You are simple and ignorant. From now on, by no means (may) you come to us. We are so many and so excellent that we don't need you.'

"But I still stand at the gate and say, 'For the love of God, let me come in tonight.' And he answers, "By no means. Go to the place of the Crosiers and beg there.'

"I tell you that if I managed patience and was not provoked, that is true joy and true virtue and the salvation of the soul."

A similar tale, although more elaborate, is told in chapter 8 of the *Little Flowers of Saint Francis*.

How often do we manage to seem patient until we're inconvenienced, until things go badly for us? How much patience and/or humility do we each have then? For most of us, I suspect that's not very much. It's amazing sometimes just how little it takes to make people lose their abilities to cope with people in a calm and loving way.

I always hate to pray for patience, because when I do situations arise in which I desperately need to have that virtue in abundance. Patience is like a muscle; it only grows when it is used. God, good Father that He is, gives us the things we ask for.

May God grant us always to grow steadily in both patience and humility. May we have those virtues in abundance during challenging times in our lives, not only for our own sakes, but, more importantly, for the sake of those people around us during those difficult times. May our actions in those difficult times not give a bad example that would turn people away from God.

Caput XIV: De paupertate spiritus

Beati pauperes spiritu, quoniam ipsorum est regnum caelorum (Mt 5,3). Multi sunt, qui orationibus et officiis insistentes multas abstinentias et afflictiones in suis corporibus faciunt, sed de solo verbo, quod videtur esse iniuria suorum corporum vel de aliqua re, quae sibi auferretur, scandalizati continuo perturbantur. Hi non sunt pauperes spiritu; quia qui vere pauper est spiritu, se ipsum odit et eos diligit qui eum percutiunt in maxilla (cfr. Mt 5,39).

Concerning poverty of spirit

Blessed are the poor in spirit, for theirs is the kingdom of heaven (Matthew 5:3). There are many who make prayers and offices, stand much fasting and affliction in their bodies, but from a single word which seems to harm their bodies or from another thing which is taken from them, they are troubled and endlessly scandalized. These are not poor in spirit, because one who is truly poor in spirit hates himself and loves the person who strikes him in the jaw. (Matthew 5:39)

Reflection on poverty of spirit

Blessed are the poor in spirit, for theirs is the kingdom of Heaven (Matthew 5:3). Anyone who grew up Christian has heard the Beatitudes many times. There is the old joke that the Beatitudes are Attitudes one should Be.

Francis, like the great saints who came before and after him, understood this first statement in the Beatitudes as a divinely revealed truth from the Lord that we disregard to the great peril of our souls. Jesus became poor for our sake, as Paul wrote in the eighth chapter Second Corinthians. Our Lord didn't speak merely a pious platitude when he taught, in Matthew 19:24, how hard it is for the rich to enter the kingdom of heaven.

(without being Holier-than-Thou)

The Gospels, indeed the entire New Testament, over and over again, shows the practice and praise of poverty. Jesus was born in a stable. He was raised in the poor town of Nazareth. During his ministry, he spoke of foxes having dens, but the Son of Man having no place to lay His head (Matthew 8:20, Luke 9:58). He rode triumphantly into Jerusalem on a borrowed ass. The Last Supper was held in a room of someone else's house. And after His crucifixion, He was laid to rest in a tomb that was donated. Jesus was poor. To follow Him faithfully, we need to take up our cross, deny ourselves, and follow Him as we find Jesus saying in Matthew 16, Mark 8, and Luke 9.

But our age doesn't want to hear any of this. People, as a rule, don't think of poverty as a virtue. In fact, we tend to believe poverty, in all forms, is something to be eliminated at all costs. "Poor" is, in our age, synonymous with "backward" and "loser". But that isn't the only thing wrong with the spirit of our age.

While secular Franciscans do not take vows of poverty, we do live within the spirit of Lady Poverty, trying to be good stewards of the resources we have in order to serve the needs of the poor and to advance the spread of the Gospel of Jesus Christ.

Yet, none of this deals with this admonition, except as background.

Francis said, *There are many who make prayers and offices, stand much fasting and affliction in their bodies, but from a single word which seems to harm their bodies or from another thing which is taken from them, they are troubled and endlessly scandalized. These are not poor in spirit, because one who is truly poor in spirit hates himself and loves the person who strikes him in the jaw.*

The offices of which Francis spoke were, of course, the appointed services of prayer throughout the day, known then by their Latin names; matins (prayed during the night), lauds (at dawn), prime (at 6 a.m.), terce (at 9 a.m.), sext (at noon), none (at 3 p.m.), vespers (at the lighting of the evening lamps), and compline (right before going to bed). Largely, the offices consist of the recitation of psalms, scripture readings, and prayers. To keep this schedule of devotions is to center one's life on worshipping God. The apostles kept the Jewish schedule of prayers (see Acts 10:3, 16:25) and the Christian liturgy of the hours developed from that. To add periods of personal prayer and other devotions to this schedule of formal prayer is a remarkable daily commitment of time to the praise and worship of God.

To fast regularly and to deny ourselves pleasures for the love of God is a good, powerful, and scriptural spiritual practice, especially when linked to prayer. This too is very much part of the Franciscan spiritual practice, just as praying the Office is.

Francis wasn't denying any of this. What Francis was saying is that the external observances of the faith, no matter how rigorous and faithfully observed, are worse than meaningless unless both one's heart and way of living is right with God. No matter how much we do for God, unless we make Jesus Christ the true Lord of our lives, unless we give Him control of everything we are and have, including our reactions to events in our lives, we are not poor in spirit. The poor in spirit will possess the Kingdom of Heaven. Our salvation depends on Jesus being truly the Lord of our lives, not just in words, but in fact, not just on Sunday, but every day and every moment of our lives.

May God grant us the grace to truly allow Jesus be the Lord and Master of our lives!

Caput XV: De pace

Beati pacifici, quoniam filii Dei vocabuntur (Mt 5,9). Illi sunt vere pacifici, qui de omnibus, quae in hoc saeculo patiuntur, propter amorem Domini nostri Jesu Christi in animo et corpore pacem servant.

Concerning peace

Blessed are the peacemakers, for they shall be called the sons of God (Matthew 5:9). Those are true peacemakers who having endured all things in the world, for the sake of the love of Our Lord Jesus Christ, maintain peace in the spirit and body.

Reflection concerning peace

There's a theme developing here. Let's review several of the admonitions we've seen so far.

To the servant of God, nothing should be displeasing except sin. No matter which way another sins, the servant of God should not be disturbed or angry, except out of charity because he gathers a treasure of blame to himself (Romans 2:5). That servant of God who is not angered or disquieted by anything, on his own behalf, lives correctly without property. He is blessed who keeps nothing for himself, but renders *to Caesar that which are Caesar's, and to God that which are God's. (*Matthew 22:21)

The servant of God is not able to learn how much patience and humility he possesses in himself while he himself is satisfied. However, when the time will come that those who ought to satisfy him act in contradiction to him, he has then that much patience and humility and no more.

Blessed are the poor in spirit, for theirs is the kingdom of heaven (Matthew 5:3). There are many who make prayers and offices, stand much fasting and affliction in their bodies, but from a single word which seems to harm their bodies or from another thing which is taken from them, they are troubled and endlessly scandalized. These are not poor in spirit, because one who is truly poor in spirit hates himself and loves the person who strikes him in the jaw. (Matthew 5:39)

And now, we have this:

Blessed are the peacemakers, for they shall be called the sons of God (Matthew 5:9). Those are true peacemakers who having endured all things in this age, for the sake of the love of Our Lord Jesus Christ, maintain peace in the spirit and body.

This admonition is the only time that I can recall that Francis, or his early biographers, uses the word "pacificus", i.e. peace-maker, or any of the grammatical inflections of that word, if not speaking of the name one of the brothers, Pacificus.

Yes, Francis did, probably, forbid the members of the Third Order to take up lethal weapons against anyone or even to carry such weapons. We know, for sure, that prohibition exists in the 1221 rewrite of that rule done by Cardinal Ugolino when the Cardinal put the primitive rule of the Brothers and Sisters of Penance in more legal language to submit it to the Holy See for approval. That single line in the Third Order Rule, more than anything else, put an end to the bloody wars between rival Italian cities. The vast number of people who entered the Franciscan Third Order, and were thus prohibited under the Rule from bearing arms, reduced the number of available fighters for those armed conflicts. Without the soldiers, there could be no wars. Eventually, the Vatican would have to insist, under the concept of a 'just war', upon a provision to allow Franciscan men to serve in armed conflicts if required by the Holy See for the good of the Church. But that's another story, entirely.

Yes, in *Legend of the Three Companions*, chapter 9, it's recorded: "Certainly, the Bishop of the city of Assisi, to whom the man of God (Francis) frequently went to for counsel, received him (Francis) kindly in person, and said, 'Alas, it seems as hardship to me, your mode of living to own nothing in this world.' To this the saint said, 'If we were to possess things, we must possess weapons to defend ourselves, inasmuch as from it (possessions) arises conflict and strife and we should in many ways be hindered from loving God and our neighbor. Therefore, we wish to possess nothing temporal in this world.' The bishop was greatly pleased with these words of God's servant."

Still, I can't recall a single time otherwise in the writings of St. Francis or the early biographies of Francis that the subject of peacemaking, or maintaining peace by avoiding conflict or shunning the means of conflict, appears. Francis did speak often about peace being a gift of God. We've already seen some of those passages.

The so-called "Peace" prayer, attributed to Francis, begins, "Lord, make us instruments of your peace." But, popular belief aside, that prayer most definitely wasn't written by Francis of Assisi. That prayer didn't even come to public awareness until 1912 when it was printed in French in a small French spiritual periodical *La Clochette,* as an anonymous work.

So that leaves us with only this: the true peacemaker, I'm convinced Francis would argue, is the person who is poor in spirit, having made Jesus his/her true Lord; the person who is patient and humble in all circumstances; who cheerfully renders to God all things that belong to God.

May God grant each of us to become true peacemakers for our age!

Caput XVI: De munditia cordis

Beati mundo corde, quoniam ipsi Deum videbunt (Mt 5,8). Vere mundo corde sunt qui terrena despiciunt, caelestia quaerunt et semper adorare et videre Dominum Deum vivum et verum mundo corde et animo non desistunt.

Concerning cleanliness of heart

Blessed are the clean in heart, for they shall see God (Matthew 5:8). Truly, they are clean in heart who, without ceasing, despise the earthly, strive for heavenly things, and always adore and contemplate the Lord God, living and true.

Reflection on cleanliness of heart

Francis loved the Beatitudes. He quoted them frequently to those he spoke to. You've seen so far that he's quoted several of the Beatitudes in these admonitions.

You've probably heard dozens of sermons over the years about purity of heart. Heaven knows there has been more written over the centuries about purity of heart, more attempts at explaining what Jesus meant than one person could possibly read in an entire lifetime. And much of it, at least much of what I've read of that tremendous mountain of writing, over the years, misses the mark.

Francis wisely distilled this down to just this: *Truly, they are clean in heart who, without ceasing, despise the earthly, strive for heavenly things, and always adore and contemplate the Lord God, living and true.*

Paul advised the Philippians (Phil. 4:8), to think on things that were good, honest, true, pure, lovely, and of good report, on virtues and praiseworthy things. That's still good advice.

The problem is that we lose sight of God, and let other things creep into our minds. Francis had a good solution to this. Bonaventure, in *Major Life*, Part 1, chapter 5, says Francis remarked, "I want my brothers to work and be kept busy. If they are idle, their hearts or tongues will soon be busy with unlawful topics." In *Rule of 1221*, Chapter 7,

Francis wrote "All brothers must work at doing good, as it has written, 'Always be doing good so that when the devil comes, he finds you occupied.' (St. Jerome, Epistle 125) and 'Idleness is the enemy of the soul' (St. Anslem, Epistle 49). The servant of God must always either be praying or doing good works."

God grant that we may be truly clean in heart, ceaselessly contemplating and adoring God!

Caput XVII: De humili servo Dei

Beatus ille servus (Mt 24,46), qui non magis se exaltat de bono, quod Dominus dicit et operatur per ipsum, quam quod dicit et operatur per alium. Peccat homo, qui magis vult recipere a proximo suo, quam non vult dare de se Domino Deo.

Concerning the humble servant of God

Blessed is that servant (Matthew 24:46) who does not praise himself more for the good which the Lord says and has worked through him than in what He says and has worked through others. The man sins who wishes to receive more from his neighbor than he, himself, wishes to give to the Lord God.

Reflection on the humble servant

Everything good that we do is an act of God through us. None of it is a cause for our feeling pride. Yet, we all too often do feel pride. Further, we want to be praised for the good we do. It's something that we need to lay aside, but that's not easy to do. Francis knew that.

In *Rule of 1221*, Chapter 17, Francis said, "We must be on our guard against pride."

In *Major Life*, Part 1, Chapter 6, Bonaventure tells us, "The saint had a horror of pride which is the cause of all evil and of disobedience which is its worst offspring."

Francis' point, the point he made in another admonition, is that to rejoice and praise the Lord because of the actions of others is nothing but giving God the glory for what He's done through other people.

In *Legend of the Three Companions,* chapter 14, Francis is quoted as saying, "The behavior of the brothers among the people must be such that all who see or hear them may glorify our heavenly Father and praise Him devoutly."

It's a good thing to praise God for the good actions of others. What is wrong, to the point of being sinful, is to expect the people around us to praise God for what He does through us, by praising us, more than we're willing to praise God for what He does through our neighbors. In Francis' words this is wishing "to receive more from his neighbor than he, himself, wishes to give to the Lord God."

While Francis wasn't a trained theologian, he was deeply in love with God and he knew the human heart.

May God grant us the grace to always be willing to give more to God than we expect from our neighbors!

Caput XVIII: De compassione proximi

Beatus homo, qui sustinet proximum suum secundum suam fragilitatem in eo, quod vellet sustineri ab ipso, si in consimili casu esset (cfr. Gal 6,2; Mt 7,12). Beatus servus, qui omnia bona reddit Domino Deo, quia qui sibi aliquid retinuerit *abscondit* in se *pecuniam Domini* Dei *sui* (Mt 25,18) et *quod* putabat *habere, auferetur ab* eo (Lc 8,18).

On compassion for one's neighbor

Blessed is the man who supports his neighbor according to his fragility in the same way he wishes to be supported if he were in the like position

(Galatians 6:2, Matthew 7:12). Blessed is the servant who renders all goods to the Lord God because he who retains anything *hides his Lord's money* (Matthew 25:18) in himself and what he thinks *to have shall be taken from him* (Luke 8:18).

Reflection on compassion for one's neighbor

Francis never gave totally new advice. Instead, he always called us to be faithful to the Gospel of Jesus Christ and to the historic teaching of the Church. In the first part of this admonition, Francis merely combined two separate teachings. Jesus gave us the "golden rule", as recorded in the seventh chapter of Matthew; whatever you would have people do to you, do this to them. Paul advised the Galatians to bear one another's burdens.

This wasn't the only time Francis gave this advice. In *Letter to All the Faithful*, Francis wrote, "he (the man in authority) should do mercy for each of his brothers as he would wish them to have with him if he were in a similar position."

Let's come back to this admonition: *Blessed is the servant who renders all goods to the Lord God because he who retains anything hides his Lord's money (Matthew 25:18) in himself and what he thinks to have shall be taken from him (Luke 8:18).*

(without being Holier-than-Thou)

Francis returns to his theme of surrendering everything to God. We've seen that repeatedly in the *Admonitions.*

May God grant us all the blessedness of living out the "golden rule" and of letting Jesus be the true Lord of our lives by surrendering everything we have, all we are, to Him!

Caput XIX: De humili servo Dei

Beatus servus, qui non tenet se meliorem, quando magnificatur et exaltatur ab hominibus, sicuti quando tenetur vilis, simplex et despectus, quia quantum est homo coram Deo, tantum est et non plus. Vae illi religioso, qui ab aliis positus est in alto et per suam voluntatem non vult descendere. Et *beatus ille servus* (Mt 24,46), qui non per suam voluntatem ponitur in alto et semper desiderat esse sub pedibus aliorum.

On the humble servant of God

Blessed is the servant who does not hold himself better when he is extolled and exalted by men than when he is held to be vile, simple and despicable. Because what a man is before God, he is only that, and no more. Woe to that religious who is placed in high position by others and who, through his own desire, is not willing to descend. *Blessed is that servant* (Matthew 24:46) who is not raised to high places through his own desire and always desires to be beneath the feet of others.

Reflection on the Humble Servant

What a man is before God, he is only that and no more. Francis managed to cut right to the core of the issue. No matter whether the people around us think us to be praiseworthy or good-for-nothing, all that really counts is who God knows we are. We're no different in the eyes of God when we're praised than when we're despised by men. Francis didn't want us to see ourselves as different under either of those circumstances, either. We must know ourselves as well as God knows us. Francis, in a later admonition, will have good advice about how to accomplish this self-knowledge.

But for now, he comes back to his theme of humility among leaders. "*Blessed is that servant* (Matthew 24:46) who is not raised to high places through his own desire and always desires to be beneath the feet of others." We've already seen Francis requiring in *Rule of 1221,* "The ministers must remember they do not have a right to serve the brothers...they must lay it aside without objection the moment they are instructed to do so."

This advice encompasses humility, poverty, and self-knowledge. We are who we are in God's sight. If we are to let Jesus truly be Lord of our lives, then everything we have, including our ways of serving

Him, are His. No matter what job we have before us, we are always no more than who we are in the eyes of God.

May the Lord grant us to see ourselves as Our Loving Father sees us!

Caput XX: De bono et vano religioso

Beatus ille religiosus, qui non habet iucunditatem et laetitiam nisi in sanctissimis eloquiis et operibus Domini et cum his producit homines ad amorem Dei cum gaudio et laetitia (cfr. Ps 50,10). Vae illi religioso, qui delectat se in verbis otiosis et vanis et cum his producit homines ad risum.

On the honest and untrustworthy religious

Blessed is that religious who has no pleasure or joy except in the most holy pronouncements and works of the Lord and with this leads men to the love of God with joy and gladness (Psalm 50:10). Woe to that religious who delights in empty and vain words and with this leads men to laughter.

Reflection on honest religious

On the surface, this seems to be only a slightly different take on the "good works must follow knowledge" admonition. Yet, it's far more than just that.

Francis is clear on the value of holy joy. In Celano's *Second Life*, Chapter 88, Francis said, "The Devil, in that moment, especially rejoices when he is able to steal spiritual joy from the servant of God...But when the heart is filled with spiritual joy, the Serpent vainly streams forth deadly poison." Later in the same chapter, this is said of Francis, "The Saint was eager for the joyful song to emerge from his heart and to preserve in his soul the unction and oil of gladness."

Nehemiah 8:10 says "the joy of the Lord is our strength." While Nehemiah was addressing the Jewish people with those words, that phrase could have been the theme song of Francis. Book 1, chapter 29, of Celano's *First Life,* says of Francis, "For he was moved beyond the understanding of men when he spoke your name, holy Lord, and at once emerged in joyful melody and full of most pure charm so that he seemed to be a man from another world."

And yet, this image of Francis is tempered by the account found in *Mirror of Perfection,* chapter 96. To put this in context, immediately before the passage that follows, Francis is reprimanding a brother for going around wearing a sad face. Francis tells the brother that it is wrong to show anyone a sad and gloomy face, that one's sorrow should be reserved for times when one is private with God. But that a cheerful face, as much as we're able to do so, should always be shown to others. And then the passage continues in this way: "By no means should it be understood or supposed that our father (Francis), an admirer of all things mature and earnest, wished this joy to be shown through laughter or even excessive empty words, whereas through these is not shown spiritual joy, but in fact emptiness and foolishness. No indeed, he particularly detested laughter and idle words in the servant of God. In fact, he (Francis) preferred them neither to laugh nor to furnish the least occasion for others to ridicule. In one of his admonitions, he (Francis) gave a clear expression of the nature of spiritual joy in a servant of God. He said this: 'Blessed is that religious who has no pleasure or joy except in the most holy pronouncements and works of the Lord and with this leads men to the love of God with joy and gladness. Woe to that religious who delights in empty and vain words and with this leads men to laughter.'"

That passage continues: "By a joyful face, then, it is understood as passion and care as well as the orderly arrangement and preparation of the mind and the body to the willing production of all good things. Through this passion and disposition people are more greatly challenged (to the performance of good deeds) than by the good acts (by) themselves. However, if an act, no matter how good it was, does not seem to have been done both willingly and with passion, it produces great offense instead of challenging (others) to good (acts). And for that reason, he was unwilling to see a gloomy face, which often fetches and introduces an attitude of the mind and a laziness of the body. He (Francis) chiefly loved seriousness and maturity in face and in all members and senses of the body, in himself and others; and as much as he was able he lead others in this by word and example. Indeed, he had experienced this manner of seriousness and habit of discipline to be just as the strongest of a wall and shield against the arrows of the devil; without this strong wall and shield, the soul is like a naked soldier among the most powerful and well-fortified enemy (who is) continually roused and intent on his annihilation."

That's a good deal to absorb.

Francis' joy was in the Lord. And he wanted us to take our gladness and joy from God as well. This joy and gladness should be expressed, not in laughter or an abundance of words, but in doing good works willingly and with fervor for how we do things is often more important than what we actually do. The example we give to others in how we work is important.

Further, Francis felt that the best defense against the devil is to cultivate the habit of being serious and self-disciplined while being joyful.

May we always rejoice in God, taking our joy in His words and the deeds done by Him. May we always employ that joy to lead others to Jesus, using our gifts and the example of both our work and demeanor for His honor and glory!

Caput XXI: De inani et loquaci religioso

Beatus servus, qui quando loquitur, sub specie mercedis omnia sua non manifestat et non est velox ad loquendum (cfr. Prov 29,20), sed sapienter providet, quae debet loqui et respondere. Vae illi religioso, qui bona, quae Dominus sibi ostendit, non retinet in corde suo (cfr. Lc 2,19.51) et aliis non ostendit per operationem, sed sub specie mercedis magis hominibus verbis cupit ostendere. Ipse recipit *mercedem suam* (cfr. Mt. 6,2.16) et audientes parum fructum reportant.

On the foolish and talkative religious

Blessed is the servant, who when he is spoken of, does not disclose all himself in the hope of reward, nor is he quick to speak (Psalm 29:20), but sensibly foresees what he ought to say and answer. Woe to that religious who displays the good the Lord has done to him, who does not conceal that in his heart (Luke 2:19) and doesn't show that to others by his actions, but desires to show that to men by his words for hope of great gain (Matthew 6:2). His hearers carry away insufficient reward.

Reflection on the foolish and talkative

Francis gave several very similar admonitions.

The Apostle said: "The letter kills, however the Spirit gives life." (2 Corinthians 3:6) Those are killed by the letter who only wish to know so much of the Word in order that they may be thought wise among others and to acquire great wealth to give to their family and friends. Those religious are killed by the letter who will not follow the spirit of the Holy Scriptures, but only desire to know so much of the Word to explain to others. Those are made alive by the spirit of Holy Scriptures who do not attribute to self all the letters they know or desire to know, but who by word and example return them to the Almighty Lord God, of whom is every good.

Blessed is that religious who has no pleasure or joy except in the most holy pronouncements and works of the Lord and with this leads men to the love of God with joy and gladness (Psalm 50:10). Woe to that religious who delights in empty and vain words and with this leads men to laughter.

And now, this:

Blessed is the servant, who when he is spoken of, does not disclose all himself in the hope of reward, nor is he quick to speak (Psalm 29:20), but sensibly that religious who displays the good the Lord has done to him, who does not conceal that in his heart (Luke 2:19) and doesn't show that to others by his actions, but desires to show that to men by his words for hope of great gain (Matthew 6:2). His hearers carry away insufficient reward.

In a later admonition, Francis will come back to this theme once more, with a slightly different twist. We shouldn't underestimate how deeply Francis felt about showing our spirituality in our actions instead of only in our words.

Francis admonition not to be quick to speak reminds me forcibly of James 1:19 in which James advises that we should be quick to hear and slow to speak.

I'm also reminded of Matthew 5:16, where Jesus advised us to let our light so shine before men so that they might see our good works and glorify our Father in heaven.

That God may be glorified in our actions and in our words that people may see Him in us, and want to have something of the peace and joy that comes directly from His presence in our lives, is precisely what Francis wanted for us.

May God give us the grace to have holy joy, the joy of the Lord, abundantly in our lives and for us to use that, through example more than word, to bring others into relationship with Jesus.

Caput XXII: De correctione

Beatus servus, qui disciplinam, accusationem et reprehensionem ita patienter ab aliquo sustineret sicut a semetipso. Beatus servus, qui reprehensus benigne acquiescit, verecunde obtemperat, humiliter confitetur et libenter satisfacit. Beatus servus, qui non est velox ad se excusandum et humiliter sustinet verecundiam et reprehensionem de peccato, ubi non commisit culpam.

Concerning Correction

Blessed is the servant who bears discipline, accusation and blame so patiently from others as from himself. Blessed is the servant who having been blamed, cheerfully accepts, modestly obeys, humbly confesses, and freely apologizes. Blessed is the servant who is not quick to excuse himself, and when he has not committed offense humbly accepts the shame and blame of sin.

Reflection Concerning Correction

There's a good deal here to think about. So, I'll take it a bit at a time.

Blessed is the servant who bears discipline, accusation and blame so patiently from others as from himself.

This seems to me to be inexorably bound with parts of a couple of earlier admonitions:"Blessed is the servant who does not hold himself better when he is extolled and exalted by men than when he is held to be vile, simple and despicable. Because what a man is before God, he is only that, and no more"; and "Blessed is the man who supports his neighbor according to his fragility in the same way he wishes to be supported if he were in the like position (Galatians 6:2, Matthew 7:12)".

If we are nothing more and nothing less than what we are before God, then what does it really matter who corrects our behavior; ourselves or someone else? And if it doesn't matter, then shouldn't we be patient under correction, from whatever source it comes?

Further, if we are in a community or a fraternity where everyone supports us as they would like to be supported, then any correction that comes our way will be given charitably. So, where's the difficulty?

Of course, that's a rhetorical question. People, being people, are always too ready to want mercy for themselves, while demanding justice for others. Those who live as Franciscans are not free from that tendency.

A commitment to live a life of penance following Jesus doesn't automatically make us saintly. Our vows and promises only strengthen our resolve to walk more closely with Jesus. But the grace to become saints, like all grace, is totally a gift from God. The church is not a haven for saints as much as she is a hospice for us sinners.

May God grant to each of us the gift of being open to correction, and the gift of being as gentle with our neighbors when they need correction as we wish them to be with us.

Blessed is the servant who having been blamed, cheerfully accepts, modestly obeys, humbly confesses, and freely apologizes.

1 John 1:9-10 encourages us to confess our sins because God is faithful and just. He will forgive us and cleanse us from our sins. And, as John reminds us, we're all sinners.

In *First Life*, chapter 19, Celano writes of Francis, "in order that he might reveal himself completely worthless and give an example to the rest of true confession, when he committed an offense he did not blush to publicly confess that in his preaching before all the people. No, indeed, if perchance he had an evil thought about another, or if he by chance had spoken a harsh word, he would immediately confess his sin with all humility to the one about whom he had the evil thought, begging his forgiveness. At once, his innocent conscience testified, not letting him rest, guarding itself with all care until it cured the wound of his heart and soothed his mind."

Francis knew quite well he was a sinner in the hands of a just and loving God. In Celano's *Second*

Life, chapter 86, a brother asked Francis, "Father, what is your opinion of yourself?" To which Francis replied, "It seems to me I am the greatest of sinners, because if God had pursued any criminal with such mercy, he (the criminal) would have been tenfold more spiritual than I."

God, grant us the gift of being humble enough to confess our faults, and to accept Your forgiveness and love.

Blessed is the servant who is not quick to excuse himself, and when he has not committed offense humbly accepts the shame and blame of sin.

Very few events are more of a challenge to our own sense of justice than to be in a situation where we're being blamed for things we didn't do. We're offended to the core of our being when people accuse us of errors that aren't our own. In that offense, we strike back at our accusers. This leads to anything except peace and joy among the people around us.

In the Gospels, Matthew 5:11 and Luke 6:22, Jesus tells us to count ourselves blessed when men revile us, shun or persecute us, and accuse us falsely of all manner of things, for His sake.

I can't imagine that's ever been pleasant to hear. But, as always, Francis never gives any advice unless it's grounded in the gospel. He calls us to be faithful to Jesus, even when that fidelity goes against all of our natural instincts.

If we are true servants of God, if Jesus is truly the Lord of our lives, we must take seriously part 1, chapter 7, of *Major Life* where Bonaventure quoted Francis as saying, "By no means has he perfectly renounced the world who holds on to his own opinions in the secret places of his heart."

God grant us the grace to humbly accept blame, whether we earned it or not!

Caput XXIII: De humilitate

Beatus servus, qui ita inventus est humilis inter subditos suos, sicuti quando esset inter dominos suos. Beatus servus, qui semper permanet sub virga correctionis. Fidelis et prudens servus est (cfr. Mt 24,45), qui in omnibus suis offensis non tardat interius punire per contritionem et exterius per confessionem et operis satisfactionem.

Concerning humility

Blessed is the servant who is found as humble among his subordinants as he would be among his superiors. Blessed is the servant who always continues under the rod of correction. Faithful and prudent is the servant who does not delay to punish himself for all his offenses through contrition, exteriorly by confession, and by works of satisfaction.

Reflection concerning humility

Bartholomew of Pisa once recounted a story in which Francis was asked what the three worst threats to the Order were. He didn't hesitate about answering. Francis said, "Boys, noblemen, and the learned. Boys will destroy discipline. Noblemen will destroy humility. And the learned brothers will destroy poverty."

The point is humility, discipline, and poverty all go together. As Francis said in *Praises of the Virtues* "who has one (virtue) and does not offend the others, has all."

How is a person able to be as humble among those who under him as he in the presence of those who are over him? We all have likely had the experience of working under an overbearing boss.

Francis was quite adamant that no one has the right to any position of authority at all. All positions have to be seen as equal ways of serving, with no post being more honorable than any other. No matter what job any of us have, we all serve the same Divine Master. There's no cause for pride in whatever ways we serve. So, why wouldn't we be as humble among those who report to us as we are when we're among those we report to?

Part of that ability to remain humble is firmly grounded in our self-knowledge. We know our-selves to be sinners. We continuously keep a close watch on ourselves, recognizing sins when we commit them. Being faithful, we confess our sins, do penance for them, and we take actions to make things right to any we have injured by our sins against them.

God, grant us the grace always to have an innocent conscience, like Francis had, one that will not allow us to rest until we've confessed our sins and put things right with anyone we've harmed.

Caput XXIV: De vera dilectione

Beatus servus, qui tantum diligeret fratrem suum, quando est infirmus, quod non potest ei satisfacere, quantum quando est sanus, qui potest ei satisfacere.

Concerning True Love

Blessed is the servant who has so great a love for his brothers when they are ill and cannot assist him, as well as when they are whole and can assist him.

Reflection Concerning True Love

True Love. Seems that the world is always desperately searching for that treasure, and looking everywhere but where it is to be found; looking everywhere except to Jesus who is Love itself.

The dignity of every human person is an important Christian concept. Each of us is formed "imago dei" in the image of God. God made us, and keeps us forever in His thoughts. He loved us enough to take the manhood into God, to become flesh and dwell among us, to die that we might be redeemed from our sins, and to give us the promise of eternal life in his resurrection from the dead.

I saw once a church signboard bearing the message, "God saw you when you were born. It was love at first sight." Cute concept. But the reality is that God knew us long before birth. The Psalmist tells us that He has been our God from our mother's wombs (Psalm 21:11).

Blessed is the servant who has so great a love for his brothers when they are ill and cannot assist him, as well as when they are whole and can assist him.

People have innate worth. Francis knew this. To repeat a theme, a man is who he is before God, and no more. Who are we before God? We are Beloved Children, created in His image, redeemed by His own act, sustained by His own Spirit.

Naturally, we must care for the weak, the ill, the infirm. These are our brothers and sisters.

In *Rule of 1221,* chapter 10, Francis requires that an ill brother must be cared for by his brethren with all the care that the rest should like to be given, if they were ill. That's nothing more than a practical application of the Golden Rule.

People cannot be properly seen as burdens we can dispose of. We live in a culture of death, where human life is held all too cheaply. Abortions and medically assisted euthanasia are legal in many places. Society says that if a life is inconvenient for one reason or another that it may be ended. It breaks my heart.

Blessed is the servant who has so great a love for his brothers...

God, grant us so great a love for our brothers and sisters that we may care for them as we wish to be cared for, if the situation were reversed.

Caput XXV: Item de eodem

Beatus servus, qui tantum diligeret et timeret fratrem suum, cum esset longe ab ipso, sicuti quando esset cum eo, et non diceret aliquid post ipsum, quod cum caritate non posset dicere coram ipso.

Likewise to the same purpose

Blessed is the servant who would love and fear his brother as much when he is long from him as when he is with him, and would not say to his back what he would not say, with charity, face-to-face.

Reflection on to the same purpose

My grandmother, rest her soul, told me much the same thing, "Never say anything about someone that you wouldn't say to that person. Makes life easier that way." Yet, Francis had more than making our lives easy in mind when he gave this advice.

In *Rule of 1221,* chapter 11, says of the brothers, "They are bound to love each other because the Lord says, 'This is my commandment, that you love one another as I have loved you' (John 15:12). And they must show love which they have towards one another, as the apostle says, 'Let us love not in word, neither with the tongue, but in works and truth' (1 John 3:18)."

Recall 1 John 4:7-8, Beloved, let us love each other, because love is from God. Everyone who loves is born of God, and knows God. He that doesn't love, doesn't know God for God is love. God is love. Francis knew this. He wanted us to love one another.

God, grant us the grace to love one another as much when we're together with our brothers and sisters as when we're apart, to love them because You love them, and not to see our brothers and sisters as means to our ends.

Caput XXVI: Ut servi Dei honorent clericos

Beatus servus, qui portat fidem in clericis, qui vivunt recte secundum formam Ecclesiae Romanae. Et vae illis qui ipsos despiciunt; licet enim sint peccatores, tamen nullus debet eos iudicare, quia ipse solus Dominus reservat sibi ipsos ad iudicandum. Nam quantum est maior administratio eorum, quam habent de sanctissimo corpore et sanguine Domini nostri Jesu Christi, quod ipsi recipiunt et ipsi soli aliis ministrant, tantum plus peccatum habent, qui peccant in ipsis, quam in omnibus aliis hominibus istius mundi.

In order that the servants of God honor priests

Blessed is the servant who carries faith in the clergy who live correctly according to the form of the Roman Church. And woe to those who despise them (the clergy). Even if they (the clergy) may be sinners, nevertheless he should not judge them. God reserves to Himself alone to judge them. For how great is the care they (the clergy) have concerning the most holy body and blood of Our Lord Jesus Christ they alone receive and minister to others, so much greater is the moral fault of those who sin against them (the clergy) than against all the other men of the world.

Reflection on honoring priests

There's never been an age, to the best of my knowledge, in which there has been a lack of a certain number of open and notorious sinners among the ranks of the clergy. Priests are sinners, just as the rest of humanity is. That's not excusing the sins of priests, by any means. But it is unjust to expect that just because a man has been ordained and stands *alter Christi* that he would cease to be human, with all the temptations and ability to sin that all humans face each moment of our lives.

Celano in *Second Life*, chapter 107, says: "Although he (Francis) wished his sons to be at peace with all men (Romans 12:18) as well as to show themselves to all men as unimportant, yet he taught by his words and showed by his example that they were to be especially humble to priests. In fact, he used to say, "We are sent for the assistance of the clergy for the salvation of souls so whatever may be found too little in them (the clergy) may be supplied by us. Each one will receive his reward, not according to authority, but according to his labor (1 Corinthians 3:8). Know, Brothers, the fruit of souls (Wisdom 3:13) is most pleasing to God. This can be better achieved by peace than by disagreement with the clergy. If they (the clergy) hinder the salvation of the people, the revenge is God's and He will render to them (the clergy) in time (Deut. 32:35). Therefore, be subject to prelates, as much as you are able, that no jealousy may arise. If you would be sons of peace (Luke 10:6), you will win the clergy and the people for the Lord. The Lord declares this more acceptable than to win the people (while) scandalizing the clergy. Cover their (the clergy's) lapses, supply for their many failures; and having done this, be even more humble."

Francis' respect for the members of the priesthood is all tied up with his respect for the Eucharist. In chapter 152 of *Second Life*, Celano wrote of Francis, "He (Francis) was wishing for great reverence to be shown to the hands of priests to which are assigned divine authority. He often would say, 'If it were to happen a Saint from heaven and a poor priest would meet with me at the same time, I would first show honor to the priest and rapidly go to kiss his hands. I would have said, 'Oh, wait, Saint Lawrence, because these hands touch the Word of Life (1 John 1:1).'"

The Dominican Etienes de Bourbon wrote an account of an example of St. Francis' respect for the priesthood. I have never seen the original of this letter, so I'll retell it, as opposed to quoting the translation that I've seen. Francis went into a town in Lombardy. He went to the Church to pray. A heretic, thinking to use Francis' reputation for holiness for the heretic's own purpose of drawing the people into his own heresy, came to Francis and quite truthfully, if maliciously, denounced the priest as a man who kept a concubine, adding the heretic's opinion that the priest's sins made him both contemptible and the sacraments he offered invalid. Francis, seeing the motive of the heretic, went to the priest in front of the people of that place. Francis knelt down before this sinful priest and spoke to this effect: I don't know if this man is a sinner or not. But even if he is, the efficacy of the sacraments is not impaired by his sins. A priest's hands convey the gifts of God for the benefit of the faithful. So, in respect for the One who gave this priest the authority to administer the sacraments, I kiss this man's hands.

Francis' actions, supporting the office of the priesthood, confused the heretic and all of that man's supporters. We don't know what effect it had upon the priest. I'd like to think these words brought the priest to repentance. But, we just don't know.

Francis, in his *Testament,* wrote, "God gave me, and gives me, such faith in the priests who live according to the form of the holy Roman Church on account of their orders, that even if they should persecute me, I wish to run to them. And if I had been having such wisdom, such as Solomon had, and came across the poorest priest in the world, I would not wish to preach in his parish against his will. And him (this poor priest) and all others (other priests), I wish to fear, love, and honor as my superiors. I am unwilling to consider their sins, because I discern the Son of God in them, and they (the priests) are my superiors. I do this because I cannot physically see the most high Son of God in this world, except for His most holy Body and Blood which they (the priests) receive and which they alone administer to others."

That is, for Francis, the essence of the argument: that because the ministry of the priesthood is the way that we have the real presence of Jesus with us in our age in the Eucharist, we must honor the holders of that office.

God, grant us always to love Jesus so much that we can respect and honor the office of the priesthood, regardless of the merit of the officeholder.

Caput XXVII: De virtute effugante vitio

Ubi caritas est et sapientia, ibi nec timor nec ignorantia.

Ubi est patientia et humilitas, ibi nec ira nec perturbatio.

Ubi est paupertas cum laetitia, ibi nec cupiditas nec avaritia.

Ubi est quies et meditatio, ibi neque sollicitudo neque vagatio.

(without being Holier-than-Thou)

Ubi est timor Domini ad *atrium suum* custodiendum (cfr. Lc 11,21), ibi inimicus non potest habere locum ad ingrediendum.

Ubi est misericordia et discretio, ibi nec superfluitas nec induratio.

Concerning Virtue chasing out Vice

Where there is charity and wisdom, there is neither fear nor ignorance.

Where there is patience and humility, there is neither anger nor commotion.

Where there is poverty with joy, there is neither lust nor greed.

Where there is quiet and contemplation, there is neither anxiety nor dissipation.

Where the fear of the Lord guards the house (Luke 11:21), there the enemy cannot have a place to enter.

Where there is mercy and discernment, there is neither excess nor harshness.

Reflection on Virtue and Vice

Celano, in *First Life,* chapter 115, said of Francis, "Jesus in his heart. Jesus in his mouth. Jesus in his ears. Jesus in his eyes. Jesus in his hands. Jesus in the rest of his members." This was Francis. He wanted to live, wanted us to live, entirely for Jesus, both exteriorly and interiorly; to experience the victory of a life of the supernatural joy that comes from renouncing self in order to live for God.

Remember what Francis had to say, in *Legend of Perugia*, about what the best sermon in the world is: *There is no better sermon than the practice of the virtues.* There's really not much more to say about this. It speaks for itself. This admonition, like the others, is a bit of solid practical advice from Francis to his brothers, and to us, today.

God, grant us ever to live our lives virtuously so that gentle sermons as to Your love may be read by others in an examination of our lives.

Caput XXVIII: De abscondendo bono ne perdatur

Beatus servus, qui thesaurizat *in caelo* (cfr. Mt 6,20) bona, quae Dominus sibi ostendit et sub specie mercedis non cupit manifestare hominibus, quia ipse altissimus manifestabit opera eius quibuscumque placuerit. Beatus servus, qui secreta Domini observat *in corde suo* (cfr. Lc 2,19.51).

Concerning hiding wealth lest it be lost

Blessed is the servant who treasures up in heaven (Matthew 6:20) the good that the Lord shows him, and who does not wish to show to men in hope of gain because the Most High may show His works to anyone He may please. Blessed is the servant who keeps the secrets of the Lord in his heart (Luke 2:19).

Reflection on not losing spiritual wealth

In Celano's *First Life*, Book 2, Chapter 3, it is written about the stigmata and Francis' keeping that hidden as much as possible, "Francis custom was to reveal his great secret rarely, or to no one at all, because he feared his revealing it to anyone might appear as a special affection for that person, in the way that special friends act, and that he would thus endure some loss of the grace that had been given to him. Thus, he carried it in his heart and frequently had on his lips this saying of the prophet, 'Thy words have I hidden in my heart that I may not sin against thee.' (Psalm 6:4)...For Francis had experienced that it is a large evil to make all things known to everyone and that he can't be a spiritual man whose secrets are not more perfect and more numerous than the things that can be read on his face and completely understood by men."

In Chapter 101 of *Second Life*, Celano wrote of Francis, "He knew the reward of public opinion to diminish the private conscience and that it is far more harmful to squander virtues than to be without them. He knew it was no unimportant virtue to protect what was acquired than to strive for."

Recall the following passage from an earlier admonition? *Woe to that religious who displays the good the Lord has done to him, who does not conceal that in his heart (Luke 2:19) and doesn't show that to others by his actions, but desires to show that to men by his words.*

The Franciscan life seeks to pattern ourselves on the life of selfless service to our Lord given by His Mother. In Luke 2:19, we're told that Mary kept all of the words of those shepherds, those men and boys who rushed to adore Jesus after the heavenly host appeared to them while they watched their flocks on the hills around Bethlehem that night Jesus was born. Mary pondered those words and those events in her heart. I suspect this is what Francis would have us do with the favors God showers upon us, in our lives, as well; to ponder them in our innermost being, to treasure and draw strength from them, to hold them as precious, like Mary did.

God, grant us the grace to ponder your gifts in our hearts, to contemplate them, to use them as You would have them used for Your honor and glory, to show them in our lives and not in our words.

Conclusion

Someone asked me once what it meant to be a Franciscan.

I answered that to be a Franciscan is to have answered the call of God to live a life of radical servanthood, following Jesus in the footsteps of Saint Francis of Assisi. To be a Franciscan is to take the Gospel of Jesus Christ to entirely to heart, to serve all persons as though we were serving Jesus. Francis' call was to rebuild the Church, by serving others in humility, prayer, simplicity, and penitence. This is also our call, our holy vocation.

Saint Francis' *Admonitions,* which we've just spent some time reading together, are useful, practical items of advice for living the Franciscan life. I hope this small book has been a blessing to you, dear reader.

May God continually bless you and give you His peace.